The
COMMANDER

The
COMMANDER

The Life and Times of Harry Steele

FRED LANGAN

DUNDURN
TORONTO

Cover images: Courtesy of the Steele family.
Printer: Friesens

Library and Archives Canada Cataloguing in Publication

Title: The Commander : the life and times of Harry Steele / Fred Langan.
Names: Langan, Fred, 1945- author.
Description: Includes index.
Identifiers: Canadiana (print) 20190116579 | Canadiana (ebook) 20190116587 | ISBN 9781459744622 (hardcover) | ISBN 9781459744639 (PDF) | ISBN 9781459744646 (EPUB)
Subjects: LCSH: Steele, Harry, 1929- | LCSH: Businessmen—Canada—Biography. | LCSH: Newfoundland and Labrador—Biography. | LCGFT: Biographies.
Classification: LCC HC112.5.S74 L36 2019 | DDC 338.092—dc23

1 2 3 4 5   23 22 21 20 19

We acknowledge the support of the **Canada Council for the Arts**, which last year invested $153 million to bring the arts to Canadians throughout the country, and the **Ontario Arts Council** for our publishing program. We also acknowledge the financial support of the Government of Ontario, through the **Ontario Book Publishing Tax Credit** and **Ontario Creates**, and the **Government of Canada**.

Nous remercions le Conseil des arts du Canada de son soutien. L'an dernier, le Conseil a investi 153 millions de dollars pour mettre de l'art dans la vie des Canadiennes et des Canadiens de tout le pays.

Care has been taken to trace the ownership of copyright material used in this book. The author and the publisher welcome any information enabling them to rectify any references or credits in subsequent editions.

The publisher is not responsible for websites or their content unless they are owned by the publisher.

Printed and bound in Canada.

VISIT US AT

  dundurn.com | @dundurnpress | dundurnpress | dundurnpress

Dundurn
3 Church Street, Suite 500
Toronto, Ontario, Canada
M5E 1M2

To Harry Steele, as original an entrepreneur as ever came out of Newfoundland, and his wife, Catherine, a true daughter of Newfoundland, a talented entrepreneur in her own right, and a partner in every sense of the word.

Contents

Introduction

The Commander. His title in the naval service has been used as the nickname for Harry Steele in the years since, as he built what became Newfoundland Capital Corporation from just an idea into the successful business it became. Although Harry became an entrepreneur relatively late in life, once he started on his quest, he made a success of himself in a hurry. In fact, Joey Smallwood, the first premier of Newfoundland and Labrador, once said of Harry Steele, "I never knew anyone to come so far so fast."

Harry Steele's start was as modest as they get. He was born in 1929 in Musgrave Harbour, an outport on Newfoundland's Atlantic coast. It is a place with one of the most beautiful beaches in all of Newfoundland, an out-of-the-way place sought after by tourists today, but when Harry was a child the remoteness of the village meant that the only way in was by boat. Times were rough in the 1930s, and the community lived on fishing and work in the woods. The school there had two rooms, one upstairs and one downstairs, and taught everything from the first grade through to the last year of high school.

When Harry left his hometown, he walked out through the bush that surrounded the village to the railway tracks that he picked up in the nearby town of Lewisporte. Not only was there no road into his village, there was no direct rail line to Musgrave Harbour either.

Harry's first job outside Musgrave Harbour involved digging ditches and performing other manual labour on the roads in Deer Lake in western Newfoundland. Then Joey Smallwood came to the rescue. The premier of Newfoundland created a scholarship program for Newfoundlanders who wanted to be teachers. Harry seized the opportunity and enrolled in Memorial University. He also joined the University Naval Training Division (a program set up by the Royal Canadian Navy to develop officers for the navy, which was short of men during the war). He needed both scholarships to survive. Although he did graduate from the teacher training program, Harry never did teach school. Instead, he joined the Royal Canadian Navy as a junior officer.

By the time he entered the navy full-time, Harry was married to Catherine Thornhill, an educated woman who taught music in St. John's. The young married couple went to England, where Harry trained as a communications specialist at a Royal Navy school. He learned about codes and radio frequencies, the foundations of military intelligence. He also learned about secrecy: the importance of keeping secret the knowledge he had of military intelligence operations. Harry Steele entered the world of the Cold War, where a critical job of the Royal Canadian Navy was to listen to the Russian-language transmissions of the Soviet fleet in the North Atlantic. Harry took secrecy seriously. To this day he will not speak of his work during that time except to say, "I read other people's mail."

He spent time at sea, on a variety of warships: a large cruiser, an aircraft carrier, frigates, and other types of vessels. He travelled the world, taking in many sights and different cultures. He saw poverty in West Africa and the opulence of diplomatic life in Washington, D.C., where he worked in naval intelligence.

Harry's last posting with the Royal Canadian Navy was as commander of the base at Gander, Newfoundland, where he served for four and half years. Gander was a key NATO base during the

Cold War — among other things, the base there kept an eye on submarine traffic in the North Atlantic and intercepted and deciphered radio messages from the Russian vessels in the nearby ocean.

Around this time, Harry became fascinated with the stock market, and he began to make investments, pooling knowledge and money with his brother-in-law Roland Thornhill. He was an astute student of markets, a natural. And his wife, Catherine, had a sharp eye for real estate. She discovered The Albatross Hotel in Gander and, together with Harry, bought it and made a success of it. It is the foundation of Steele Hotels today.

Harry left the navy in 1974, riled by the amalgamation of Canada's armed forces by Lester Pearson's Liberal government — an action that resulted in the loss of many military traditions. The end of Harry's military career resulted in the beginning of a new chapter in his life.

Harry began his civilian career working for Eastern Provincial Airways (EPA). The Newfoundland-based airline had its operations and head office in Gander, so Harry was already familiar with its people and operations. He worked only briefly at the airline, however, leaving after a year. His decision to depart seemed a good one, since EPA was on the ropes. Shortly thereafter, though, he had a change of heart about the airline. He learned that the Crosbie family, the owners of the company, was looking for a way out. The airline's stock price was in the basement and the Crosbies were looking to cut their losses. Harry had been picking up a sizeable number of shares since he joined the company, and at this point, he decided that he could turn the airline around. So, Harry mortgaged everything he and Catherine had and bought the airline. He was forty-nine years old.

"EPA Changes Hands … But It's Still a Newfoundlander" screamed the *St. John's Daily News* headline on November 22, 1978, when Harry bought the airline.

He ran the airline the same way Harry Steele, naval commander, would run a ship or a military base: keeping operations tight. To make the company profitable, it was crucial that costs be cut. The firm's team found a way to reduce the fuel burn of EPA's Boeing 737s by 10 percent, saving a million and a half dollars a year.

The company's other cost-cutting measures were not so obvious. One example: Eastern Provincial Airways was the first airline in Canada to become non-smoking. This change resulted in a healthier atmosphere during flights, but it also meant that the ashtrays didn't need to be cleaned after short hops. Under The Commander, EPA had the lowest cost structure in Canada.

Increasing revenue while reducing costs was a struggle, and Harry Steele fought some fierce battles in his efforts to accomplish both. The big airlines, Air Canada and CP Air, blocked his plans to expand to Montreal and Toronto; he won. Unions blocked his drive for reasonable hours and lower costs. He won that fight too.

Eventually, CP Air bought Eastern Provincial. That deal provided the capital for the growth of Newfoundland Capital Corporation (NCC), a company that Harry had established to hold some of his and Catherine's early investments. It acquired Clarke Transport; Halterm, a company with container operations in the port of Halifax; a trucking company; a firm providing ferry service on the St. Lawrence River; and Oceanex, a shipping company serving ports from Montreal to St. John's and Halifax. NCC had operations on land, at sea, and in the air. On top of all that, Harry Steele personally owned Universal Helicopters, hotels in Gander, and fishing camps in Newfoundland and Labrador. Harry's friend and business associate Seymour Schulich says Harry fished for business as much as he did for salmon.

Harry Steele's deep connections to corporate Canada meant Newfoundland Capital had a blue ribbon board of directors. Harry's business acumen was admired and sought across the country, and he joined many boards, including those of PWA (Pacific Western Airlines), Dundee Bancorp, Fishery Products International, and his dear friend Craig Dobbin's CHC (Canadian Helicopter Corporation).

Along the way, Harry invested in newspapers, magazines, and radio stations. In the 1990s there was a total re-think and re-organization of NCC. Clarke Transport, Halterm, Oceanex, and all the related transportation businesses were sold. The newspapers and magazines went too. That left a pure media play, 101 radio stations across Canada. Newcap Radio was sold in 2018.

On April 29, 1992, then governor general Ray Hnatyshyn invested Harry Steele as a member of the Order of Canada. In his comments during the ceremony, Hnatyshyn remarked: "Although he remains modest about his career achievements, this Newfoundlander had a distinguished naval career before becoming one of the leading entrepreneurs in the Maritimes. He is a generous employer and community-minded citizen whose support of various local causes in the areas of education, health care and the arts is well-known."

Along with his Order of Canada, Harry has received many other awards, including alumni of the year at Memorial University.

Joey Smallwood was right about Harry Steele. He came so far so fast. He did it through hard work and the discipline that he learned as a young man in Musgrave Harbour and as an officer in the Royal Canadian Navy. He is one of Newfoundland's most celebrated entrepreneurs and a man who has given back much to the place where he was born.

One

Musgrave Harbour

You are judged by the company you keep so pay attention.

— Harry Steele

Musgrave Harbour is a tiny, isolated outport on the northeast coast of Newfoundland. The village is on a piece of land that sticks out into the cold North Atlantic — only the ocean lies between it and Ireland. Today people come to Musgrave Harbour to walk its seven-kilometre white sand beach and look out to the Atlantic, hoping to perhaps see a passing iceberg, but these features, appreciated by modern tourists, would have been of only passing interest to the village's early inhabitants, focused as they were on eking out a living.

The village was first settled in 1834, by a family called Whiteway. The census of 1836 lists eleven members of the Whiteway clan living in Muddy Hole, as the village was originally known. That rather undignified name was changed in 1886; the name *Musgrave* honours Sir Anthony Musgrave, the governor of the British colony of Newfoundland in the early 1860s.

A true child of the British Empire, Sir Anthony was born in the West Indies and served as a colonial governor from Jamaica to Queensland in Australia, where he died in 1888. There are sixteen places around the world named for Musgrave. It is certain he never visited the village in Newfoundland named for him.

Always a poor place, Musgrave Harbour was a particularly difficult place to live during the Depression. Beaton Mouland, a childhood friend of Harry, says things were primitive in Musgrave Harbour. There was no electricity in the early days and little in the way of creature comforts: most residences had an outhouse. Mouland remembers that he and his brother Huey had to chop a lot of firewood in the summer to prepare for winter. "We had to use wood in the iron stoves because there was no electricity. No one thought of it as a hardship; that's the way life was.

"It was poor. There wasn't much money around in those days. You grew your own vegetables, and you'd have to go out in the woods to get wood to warm yourselves. You had a very nice home, but you had to put your firewood into an iron stove to keep warm."

The people of the village made their own fun, according to Mouland. "Life was very good. People used to help each other. We had nice times … out in the garden eating potatoes when the fine weather was on…. We had good times and enjoyed a little scoff together."* Mouland remembers it all with a smile on his face.

Musgrave Harbour may have been isolated, but the Steele family and everyone else in village were connected to the outside world in one way or another. One connection was the Anglo-Newfoundland Development Company. It was founded in 1903 by the two Harmsworth brothers, the British owners of London's *Daily Mail* newspaper. The forests of Newfoundland helped feed the voracious newspaper reading habits of the British public. The *Daily Mail* alone sold a million copies a

---

* While the word *scoff* might seem a bit archaic, it appears to be common parlance in Musgrave Harbour. It means to eat, of course. The English borrowed the word from the Dutch, and there is even a festival in town called the Muddy Hole Scuff and Scoff.

Harry as a babe in arms with his father, Stanley, at a lumber camp.

day in the capital of the British Empire at a time when London was the largest city in the world. The press barons worried that a war with Germany would cut off their supply of newsprint from Finland and Sweden, so they financed the construction of a mill at Grand Falls. The building of newsprint mills in Newfoundland resulted in railway construction, the construction of a new port, and work for thousands of Newfoundlanders.

Despite the work provided by the Anglo-Newfoundland Development Company's operations, most of the people in Musgrave Harbour still eked out a subsistence living. The Steeles did a bit better for themselves, but only a little. Just about every man in the village did some fishing, as did Harry's father, Stanley. His main job, though, was working in the woods. He was a contractor with the Anglo-Newfoundland Development Company. He would organize the work crews in central Newfoundland, where his wife, Katie, worked with him. Stanley had just about a hundred men working under him, and part of the deal was that he was responsible for their lodging and food. Harry's mother, born Kathleen Power and always called Katie, cooked meals for the men in the lumber camp during the logging season.

Katie and Stanley Steele had two children: Audrey and Harry. They went to a two-room school, Wesleyan Hall. Beaton Mouland recalls: "Harry was a nice young fellow. His home wasn't very far from ours. We went to school together. It was what they called Wellesley [*sic*] Hall, and the hall was up top. They used to have concerts up there at Christmas time. He was a nice young man when we were growing up together. We used to run together, run home from school together and all that stuff."

Though their son wasn't a great student, Katie recognized he was an inquisitive boy with an insatiable curiosity. She encouraged him to finish high school — many children in Newfoundland outports dropped out early to work in fish plants or go to sea. The lack of education trapped them in the life their families had lived for generations, though they may not have objected to the simple life of hard work and isolation.

His parents may have been instrumental in ensuring that Harry got an education, but he developed an early interest in business on his own. In Musgrave Harbour, there was only one place to buy things, a store run by T.W. Abbott. The shop owner fascinated the young Harry Steele. Here was someone who didn't have to fish or cut wood to make a living.

Kathleen Steele, Harry's mother.

"My grandparents, Stanley Steele and Kathleen Steele, taught my father the basic things about hard work, accountability, responsibility, honouring your word, making the best of what you have," says Peter Steele. "But that was subsistence, carving a life out of hard conditions as opposed to entrepreneurial ability. The reality was hard work.

"The entrepreneur that my father encountered as a young boy that led him toward the business side, was a gentleman known as T.W. Abbott. He was the local merchant in Musgrave Harbour, a larger-than-life figure from whom everybody bought their provisions," says Peter. "Put this in the context of the Musgrave Harbour of the day, where you had four or five hundred people who lived a subsistence existence working to get the cash through forestry and fishing to get the basics. T.W. Abbott controlled that part of the economy, consumerism and staples."

Harry saw that Abbott lived a comfortable existence in Musgrave Harbour, though he was hardly a plutocrat like the legendary oligarchs of St. John's, known as the Water Street Merchants.

The shop was simple, with wooden floors like many of the other general stores in Newfoundland's isolated outports and rural towns. Behind the cash register was a framed photograph showing two men, one smiling, the other frowning. Underneath the smiling man were the words: "I sold for cash." Written below the frowning face: "I sold for credit."

"T.W. Abbott was the first entrepreneurial person … that my father encountered. My father always loved that picture behind the cash register at T.W. Abbott's store and he referenced it numerous times over his lifetime. It resonated so much with my father that he never forgot it," says Peter Steele.

"My father saw that T.W. had a better life because he owned that business that made him a contributor and a man in charge of his own destiny. That affected my father deeply his whole life. He was the first person to show him that by being in business one could get a better material life."

Other people who had seen the wide world impressed Harry. His cousin Lloyd Cuff, who had fought overseas in the Second World War, was one such person. When the local soldiers came marching home, a record player blasted out marching music in the streets of Musgrave Harbour. Harry sat enraptured as his cousin told him of meeting the great British general, Bernard Montgomery. The veterans spoke of the war, probably not the horrors they saw, but certainly the places and people they had seen.

Harry stayed on in school, whether from ambition or because there was no work in Musgrave Harbour. He graduated high school from the two-room schoolhouse but soon was restless. There was little paid work to speak of in Musgrave Harbour.

"When we was young there were no jobs, not like it is now," says Beaton Mouland. "Back then, you had to do what you could and teach yourself. I could do anything then, painting, and I was a good carpenter. Just by looking at people. I built nine small lobster boats about twenty feet long for people doing lobster catching."

Beaton left Musgrave Harbour when he was forty-five years old and went to Gander where he worked for Catherine and Harry at The Albatross Hotel. He was the maintenance manager there for twenty years. "I was sometimes up at night-time if somebody wanted something. I could do most everything, but I wasn't allowed to do wiring because it was too dangerous. I could put a small outlet in, but that's it. But the rest I could do anything at all. Jack of all trades they used to call me." When the Steele family built a new house in Gander, Beaton worked on it as a carpenter.

Harry was loyal to his childhood friend. Beaton went to Nova Scotia to work on the Steele's house in Dartmouth. He also went to the Steele's modest condo in Florida. "Me and my wife was down there a month before Harry and Catherine come back. They were going around the world on a cruise, and I was there for a month in February," says Beaton, who still lives in a comfortable old people's home in Gander.

Despite the tough times, Harry has fond memories of growing up in Musgrave Harbour. Anyone who is as successful as he became would almost certainly be well grounded in childhood. He remembers the good times, but he also remembers the grinding poverty.

"The big thing in Newfoundland in those days was the scarcity of everything and no money. I followed a few friends of mine from Musgrave Harbour and looked for work where they went," recalls Harry. But he didn't fancy what they were doing. "You couldn't get paid any money to make a living. So, I worked for three years in Deer Lake, as a labourer on the roads. It was like going to end of the world," says Harry.

It might be a short distance on the map, but getting there involved going by boat to another village, then a long walk, a train ride on the slow-moving, narrow gauge Newfie Bullett, and then some more walking. It was tough work, though the young Harry Steele was used to work and he was strong and healthy.

While he was working in Deer Lake, Harry decided working on the roads for the rest of his life was not for him. He looked around for other things to do. First, he applied to join the Royal Canadian Mounted Police, who were new to the local population since Newfoundland had just joined Canada. The RCMP turned him down.

The Royal Canadian Navy had a recruiting office, and that was his first contact with the navy. That helped pay the freight at university, but so did a grant from Joey Smallwood, the first premier of Newfoundland, as we will see in the next chapter.

"I decided I should go back to school at Memorial University. I had to be subsidized; otherwise I would never have made it."

Harry Steele, without a doubt the most illustrious son of Musgrave Harbour, was born there on June 9, 1929. No one could have known that the son of one of the lumbermen would one day be a media baron, one who owned a few newspapers of his own, as well as numerous radio stations. Harry Steele went on to surprise everyone who knew him as a boy. He may even have surprised himself.

Like Harry Steele, Rex Murphy is a success story from Newfoundland. The two men are different, the navy man and entrepreneur versus the Rhodes Scholar and sharp-witted journalist, but the two share a love of Newfoundland, and each admires the accomplishments of the other.

Rex Murphy thinks to know Harry Steele you have to understand Newfoundland and the places like Musgrave Harbour that formed his character.

"There's a cliché, and clichés are sometimes true. I would think the key to Harry Steele if you were looking for one is Newfoundland, Musgrave Harbour and Newfoundland, in the 1930s and 1940s. They were isolated," says Rex, sitting over a light lunch of spring rolls in a Chinese restaurant by Lake Ontario in Toronto.

"He told me, and I can't remember the name of the other town where he had met this young lady, he'd walk along the railway line or the shoreline path in the winter to go down seventeen miles to visit the girlfriend. It was the hard old days and the people were so tough," says Rex.

"No one knows the thirties and forties in Newfoundland unless you've had a relation, like my father, who went through them. Steele was one of those guys, at eighty-nine now, who proves it, that nothing in the environment could ever stop him. He came out of that breed that's up around the northeast coast, the sealing captains. I think that Harry Steele would have been a sealing captain if he had been born about thirty years earlier."

Two

A Kickstart from Joey Smallwood

Seldom right. Never in doubt.
— Harry Steele

We are all part of all that we have met. A steal from the poet Tennyson, and more than true in the case of Harry Raymond Steele. We are all part of the place we were born and the era in which we grew up.

Harry Steele was a child in the Depression and came of age in the years before Newfoundland joined Canada. Proud of his roots, Harry was also determined to break free and make more of himself. He showed a streak of adventurousness when he walked out of Musgrave Harbour along the railway tracks and made his way to western Newfoundland, where he started work as a labourer on the roads in Deer Lake.

It seemed that there wasn't much of a future for him at the time. Harry could have returned to his outport home and taken up a subsistence life of fishing and working in the woods. But then opportunity presented itself, and Harry grabbed it.

Let's step back a bit. When Harry Steele was born in 1929, Newfoundland was a self-ruling Dominion, the same as Canada. The people of Newfoundland elected their representative government, which was headed by a prime minister. The Great Depression of the 1930s hit Newfoundland particularly hard. Cod prices were cut in half, and the same was true for overall exports. A quarter of the population was on government relief. The government had to borrow to help people survive.

When Newfoundland prime minister Frederick Alderdice announced in 1932 that the Dominion was so financially strapped it would have to renege on its debt, the British government was in shock. At the time, 56 percent of government revenues were paid just in interest on loans. Although Britain and Canada covered some of the debt, Newfoundland was still unable to pay the interest on the loans that it had incurred. A commission was set up to study the problem; the solution was that Newfoundland was in effect put into receivership. London would set the rules, not the elected representatives of the people of Newfoundland.

It was front-page news in the *New York Times* on November 22, 1933: "Britain to Govern Newfoundland; First Dominion to Lose Status." The story from London went on to say that Newfoundland "will lose her status as a self-governing Dominion."

The Commission of Government ruling Newfoundland took office in February of 1934. It was made up of a governor, a Brit appointed by London, and six men, three from Britain, three from Newfoundland. It was a humiliating experience for Newfoundlanders.

Throughout the Depression, Newfoundland continued to suffer, but the Second World War brought prosperity to Newfoundland. Since it was the closest point in North America to Britain and Europe, it became home to a giant air and naval base. The island teemed with well-paid soldiers, sailors, and aircrew, and Britain, Canada, and the United States poured money into military bases and airfields.

At the end of the war, there was growing dissatisfaction with being ruled from London. Britain, sucked dry by the war and close to insolvency itself, was only too willing to be rid of the responsibility for Newfoundland. There were three main choices: return Newfoundland to Dominion status; join Canada; or join the United States.

Joey Smallwood, a writer and radio broadcaster, led the camp to join Canada. Chesley Crosbie, who would later play a part in Harry Steele's life with Eastern Provincial Airways, pushed for Newfoundland to become part of the United States. The Steele family from Musgrave Harbour was on the pro-Canada side. As we all know, Smallwood won, and Newfoundland joined Canada in 1949. Enough of the history lesson.

One of the first things Premier Smallwood did was to offer three hundred dollars, quite a sum in 1949, to any high-school graduate in Newfoundland who wanted to go to Memorial University and earn a teaching degree. Harry Steele took him up on it.

"I worked for three years in Deer Lake, and then I decided I should go back to school, but I didn't have any money so I went to Memorial [University] four years in a row and I had to be sub-sidized otherwise I would never have made it," says Harry.

In addition to the Smallwood bursary, there was support from the navy, as Harry had signed on to the UNTD, the University Naval Training Division, which offered to pay for tuition in return for a promise to serve in the navy for a brief period after graduation.

During term, Harry had to live in St. John's, but every chance he had, he would return home. Christmas and other holidays, Harry would go home to Musgrave Harbour. Many times he would walk the last thirty-two kilometres from Lumsden, after arriving there by boat.

"When Dad was in Memorial University, there wasn't any road connecting Musgrave Harbour with any other parts of the island. You had to travel by boat," says Harry's oldest son, Peter, a man with a phenomenal memory, in particular when it comes to family lore.

"When he would come home at Christmas as a student he would always land at a community called Lumsden, just along the coast from Musgrave. He would be met often by his cousin Lloyd Cuff. They would walk along the beach by the salt water, and it was twenty miles. He did it because he wanted to do it, not because he had to do it."

Harry started university in 1949. Although he had accepted a bursary from the province to receive the training necessary for becoming a teacher, the prospect of becoming a schoolteacher wasn't that appealing to Harry. He enjoyed learning and the new things university life opened for him, but what lay beyond university remained a question for him.

Harry never boasted of being a stellar student. He did enough to get by. When he wrote his final exams, he was already going out with Catherine Thornhill, who had graduated from Mount Allison University and was teaching music in St. John's.

"Harry was going to come and see me after he wrote his exams. It was only about an hour, and I wasn't ready and all of a sudden the doorbell rang and who should it be? I said, 'Harry, what happened, didn't you have to write your exam?'"

"Yes, I wrote until I figured I had fifty."

"I should have known then I was making a mistake," says Catherine with a smile. "Because if it was three hours for the exam and I could get three hours and one minute, I'd take it. Opposites attract and you have them here. But somehow it has worked. Sixty-two years."

When Harry earned his Bachelor of Education in 1953, he went into the navy. On the list of naval officers serving in the Royal Canadian Navy at the time, his name stands out. He was one of the few with a B.Ed. By this time he was a married man, and joining the military meant leaving Newfoundland, where he had lived all his life, and connecting to the broader world.

Harry took to the navy like a sailor to water. Many of his fellow students from the UNTD program went into the navy to fulfill their obligations. Harry quickly realized he loved military life. It was the height of the Cold War, the standoff between the Soviet

Union and the western countries united under NATO, the North Atlantic Treaty Organization.

Joey Smallwood never knew Harry Steele when he was a student; later in life, when Harry was a successful businessman, the former premier knew him well. There is no record of whether Joey Smallwood took credit for Harry Steele's success.

Three

In the Navy

People would be well advised to go on
receive sometimes rather than transmit.
— Harry Steele

The navy was made for Harry, and in many ways, it made him. The boy from Musgrave Harbour embraced the discipline of the navy while he was at Memorial University. Once he graduated, Harry started a life at sea almost right away.

September 18, 1952, is recorded as the starting date of active service for acting sub-lieutenant H.R. Steele on the Naval List, the official record of every officer serving in the Royal Canadian Navy. Formerly a classified document, the list is now available online: navalandmilitarymuseum.org/archives/projects/the-navy-list.

Harry was assigned first to HMCS *Cabot*, the naval headquarters in St. John's (onshore naval depots, like actual vessels, carry HMCS). According to the Naval List, the first ship he was assigned to was HMCS *Ontario*, a light cruiser, the largest warship (apart from aircraft carriers) in the Royal Canadian Navy, and the most powerful ship in the RCN at the time. In 1951 it took Princess Elizabeth and her husband, the Duke of Edinburgh, as Prince Philip was known until 1957, from Sydney, Nova Scotia, to Newfoundland during the Royal Visit.

When Harry joined the *Ontario* as a junior officer, it went on a training cruise from Esquimalt in British Columbia across the Pacific to Australia and New Zealand.

By the middle of 1954, Harry was serving on HMCS *Magnificent*, an aircraft carrier known affectionately to her crew as the *Maggie*. Harry was on the *Magnificent* for a little more than a year, but missed the ship's biggest deployment, bringing Canadian peacekeeping troops to police the Suez Crisis, the initiative that won the Nobel Peace Prize for future prime minister Lester Pearson.

That was a one-off assignment for the Royal Canadian Navy. It was the height of the Cold War, and the navy's main task was patrolling the North Atlantic, keeping an eye on Soviet vessels, from spy ships disguised as trawlers to submarines. That was the world Harry was about to enter.

When he left the *Magnificent*, Harry was posted to a specialized Royal Navy training school in the naval port of Portsmouth, England. The school, called HMS *Mercury*, specialized in communications.

Harry was there for the better part of a year, and Catherine went with him. She recalls that she enjoyed her time in England. "We went to England not long after we were married. I loved it." She gave up teaching in St. John's to go with Harry. They didn't have children at the time. Their son Peter would be born in September of 1956, by which time they were back in Canada.

What Harry learned in England would shape the rest of his naval career. Captain (Ret'd) Edward "Ted" Kelly was a senior officer in the RCN and describes how junior officers moved on to a specialty once they gained a bit of seniority. "In those days, after you served at sea for a while, the next step was to specialize in some facet of the operations, and the areas of specialization in those days were communications, navigation and direction, gunnery, or torpedo anti-submarine fields. Harry was interested in communications. So he went to England and did what was called

A "jackstay" transfer from HMCS *Magnificent* to HMCS *Ontario*.

a long course, which meant that at the end he was a specialist in communications," says Ted.

When Harry returned to duty at sea, it was aboard HMCS *Nootka*, the most modern of the Tribal-class destroyers, a group that included the *Haida* and the *Huron*. These other ships had distinguished themselves in the Second World War. The *Nootka*, built in Halifax, entered service just after the war. Harry joined as the communications officer in charge of all radio traffic, trained in what he calls "reading other people's mail," that is, monitoring the signals sent from other ships, in particular Soviet vessels and other ships of the Warsaw Pact, the military alliance headed by the Soviet Union.

All Tribal-class destroyers were named after Indigenous bands, and the *Nootka* took the name of a First Nation on the coast of British Columbia. During Harry's time on the *Nootka*, the ship was at the centre of an Escort Group patrolling with the Atlantic Fleet of the Royal Canadian Navy.

Serving on a Tribal was a rite of passage in the RCN. The ships were well armed and fast: The *Nootka*'s maximum speed was 36.5 knots, the equivalent of 67.6 kilometres an hour. It was one of the first two Canadian naval ships to circumnavigate the world, though that did not take place on Harry's watch.

Harry's next ship was HMCS *Sault Ste. Marie*, a minesweeper that had seen service in the Second World War. While he was serving on the *Sault Ste. Marie*, Harry was promoted to lieutenant. Although the naval rank has the same name as an army rank, a naval lieutenant outranks an army officer with the same designation.

In 1959 Harry was posted to the RCN's headquarters in Halifax, HMCS *Stadacona*. No one, especially Harry, will tell you what he was doing there, but one can only assume he was involved in the communications monitoring operations of the naval base.

The following year he moved to another naval base in Nova Scotia, HMCS *Cornwallis*, the centre for training new recruits. There, Harry's specialized skills and training as a naval communication specialist would have been put to good use.

Flight deck of HMCS *Magnificent* with U.S. Navy Blimp.

Harry as a junior officer in 1954 by the guns of the cruiser HMCS *Ontario*, the largest ship ever to sail in the Royal Canadian Navy.

The Naval List has Harry back at sea aboard HMCS *Fort Erie* in 1961. An older and slower vessel from the Second World War, the *Fort Erie* was a River-class frigate, ordered during the war as an improvement on the corvettes, which were the backbone of the wartime Royal Canadian Navy. *Fort Erie*'s top speed was around twenty knots. Like the corvette, it was an anti-submarine vessel, but the *Fort Erie* was faster than a corvette, better armed, and equipped with more accurate ways of aiming depth charges at submarines.

We know a lot about Harry's posting on this ship because of the recollections of a fellow officer, Bill Shead. "Harry and I were shipmates on HMCS *Fort Erie*. I joined the ship in June of 1960 and left maybe one and a half or two years later. This was the squadron leadership for the 7th Squadron, and Harry was the squadron's communications officer," says Bill.

With that position came a lot of responsibility. All communications operations of the other ships reported to Harry. The job was to monitor traffic at sea. A vitally important activity even in relatively quiet times, these operations were even more crucial at that time — the apex of tension in the Cold War. The Soviet leader, Nikita Khrushchev, tested the resolve of the newly elected American president, John F. Kennedy, by sending missiles to Cuba. The Berlin Wall was built that year. The American-backed Bay of Pigs invasion of Cuba failed.

NATO ships patrolling the North Atlantic, including those of the Royal Canadian Navy, were on full alert. Lieutenant Harry Steele was busy decoding messages and monitoring Russian-language radio traffic.

"We had a section of communications called radiomen supplementary, and these were radiomen who basically listened for Russian traffic or enemy traffic on special frequencies in a special section of the ship," says Bill.

"These radiomen, in some cases, had special training in the Russian language. They were basically off by themselves, unlike all the other communicators, who would be responsible for standing their watch in the communications centre for example. The radiomen supplementary who were doing this spook job, if you want to call it that, had one area that they went to and the communications officer was generally the only one that went in there to see what was going on," says Bill.

"Harry wasn't only responsible for monitoring communications; he also supervised the work of those creating encryptions because most of our traffic went out encrypted. We had confidential books and codes that we had to set, and if we were receiving traffic with a high-security requirement, the message would come in encoded and then it would have to be decoded, which went to either one of the senior communicators on board. Harry would have to go up and use the Canadian version of the Enigma machine.

"We saw an awful lot of Russian traffic, particularly fishermen, and when there's fishermen you'll also find that there's usually a Russian spook ship — a spy ship as they were called. They were pretty overt because they had to be fairly large with big antenna arrays and sometimes dishes, so you knew it was more than a trawler," says Bill.

To this day, both Bill and Harry are pretty tight-lipped about any incidents that occurred during this period. They signed the Official Secrets Act, and they still take it seriously.

There was more to life on Canadian ships than reading radio traffic. There was the routine, and that's when men got to know each other.

Bill Shead recalls: "Harry often sat watches, and I was his second officer of the watch while I was under training. Each watch was four hours. When the ship was underway, you were responsible for the navigation of the ship; you would investigate anything like a man overboard and, if necessary, conduct a rescue. Generally, when you are on watch you would keep the position fixed if you were in pilotage waters or in areas where you could actually take a fix. Sometimes, in those days, the only way you could take a fix was by maintaining a dead reckoning of the ship's track from one fix to another.*

"In the morning you would get up, and you would fix the ship's position with the star fixes or things like that, and then you'd predict its track depending on the course and speed of the

---

* They would take the "fix" or location using a sextant, an instrument first used by the Royal Navy in the early eighteenth century.

ship and then around noon you'd take another sight, this time probably from the sun and you'd fix the ship's position again. Nowadays, it's all GPS, and people don't know anything about fixing a ship's position."

Communications was Harry's main responsibility. "Harry was responsible for all the communications in the ship and in the squadron. In those days, we didn't have computers, and we relied a lot on radio frequency traffic, high frequency when we were far out at sea, UHF when we were in close company, and VHF for a little bit longer range.

"Close company means 'line of sight.' For UHF, your range for radio is probably just over the horizon, whereas with high frequency, you have a longer radio wave and you can transmit radio internationally. So, if we were off the east coast of Africa, we would use high-frequency radio to send communications traffic back to Canada. But if we were travelling with a group of ships, our normal method of communication would have been on the UHF, so the range of our communication would only remain probably within an area of twenty miles."

Ted Kelly is a retired captain who served in the same squadron as Harry, though never on the same ship. "I knew him, of course. That was in the 7th Squadron of frigates back in the early 1960s. Harry was the squadron communications officer serving on the *Fort Erie*, which was his squadron commander's ship. In those days, there was double-duty: they were the ship's officer in the squadron commander's ship and also had the responsibility for the squadron itself in their particular specialty. Harry, being a communications specialist officer, would have been responsible for all that.

"In those days, each ship had a communications department comprised of three different elements of communicators: one was the signalmen, who operated visual signals like lights, semaphore, flags, and all of that. The other was the radiomen who handled all the radio communications. There was a broadcast, and all the transmission in those days was by Morse. Then also they had the radio supplementary branch, which were the people who monitored communications circuits around the world that was part of the Cold War."

That meant Harry and his team were listening for signals from Russian submarines and all communications from sources that they knew had material or information that was directed toward the Russian Fleet operations.

"The Canadian navy in those days drew upon its wartime experience where it was principally an anti-submarine convoy escort. It formed the principal task of the Canadian navy, and we got pretty good at it, and, as a result, our post-war contribution to the NATO alliance was directed toward anti-submarine, which was considered to be the major threat in those days," says Captain Kelly.

"I knew Harry more by observation than by close collegial association. He was a well-known and well-respected naval officer. As you might expect, he had a strong personality and he cut a figure; he had a reputation. He knew how to handle people; he was particularly good at leading people."

Harry also served in a non-technical role in the squadron. Harry was the wardroom wine caterer. Though never a big drinker, Harry was in charge of making sure the officers were supplied with wine and liquor. The ship was a duty-free zone of its own. When it entered a foreign port, it would be Harry's job to buy duty-free liquor and wine from chandlers — the people who supply ships, both warships and merchant vessels. It wasn't only the officers he was buying for. In those days, the Royal Canadian Navy still served up a "tot" of rum — two-and-a-half ounces of dark rum — to the sailors every day, a tradition carried over from the Royal Navy and only stopped in 1972.

The navy is the most formal branch of the Canadian military. There is a reason for it: to maintain discipline at sea in a crowded ship demands sticking to the rules, and tradition and proper dress are part of those rules, staying neat and civilized when the easy thing to do would be to let things go. Discipline and order. That extended to relatively formal dining habits.

"We were a pretty tight boardroom because on a frigate we were a dozen officers and we were a senior ship, so we set an example in terms of dress and deportment and what we did in the wardroom was traditional," says Bill Shead.

"Let me tell you this story about Harry. I think it exemplifies his philosophy of life and why he has succeeded the way he has," says Bill. "In our first days at sea we went to Bermuda, and that was the first time we had the opportunity of re-stocking the wardroom bar. So Harry, being the wardroom wine caterer, went ashore and got all the booze and brought it back, making sure the ship was well-stocked.

"One day this executive officer who was president of the wardroom asked, 'Harry, how come we have so many different varieties of Scotch in the bar?'

"You know, in the wardroom there were maybe ten or twelve officers and not all of them drank Scotch but we had about seven different brands, and Harry said to the executive officer, generally known as *number one,* 'I'd hate like hell to have a guest come aboard this ship and ask for a drink that we don't have.' So there was his approach to his service in a nutshell."

A navy ship was also a floating Canadian embassy, serving as a reception space wherever it went, whether Lagos or Antwerp. "Because we were responsible for hosting dignitaries in foreign ports, we in the wardroom had a fairly good supply of wines and spirits, which Harry would buy, and we would use that for the hospitality that we would have to extend on official occasions. Wardroom members could buy liquor at duty-free prices," says Bill Shead.

He describes the formal dinners at sea and in port that made the long tours at sea more tolerable. "If we had a mess dinner, you'd have soup and sherry, and then you'd have the main course with white and red wine, and then you'd have port afterward and maybe liqueurs after that. It sounds like a lot, but over the space of a few hours, it really wasn't. Nobody got blind-eyed drunk and certainly not on the *Fort Erie*."

HMCS *Gatineau* was the pride of the Canadian fleet when Harry served on it in 1963. The *Gatineau* was a modern Canadian destroyer; its sleek design was unlike anything seen in the RCN before. While serving on the *Gatineau*, Harry was promoted to the rank of lieutenant-commander. The following year, he served on a sister ship, HMCS *Restigouche*, a vessel of identical design. The Cold War continued, Canadian ships patrolled the North Atlantic, and the communications officer was busy reading Russian radio traffic and sending encrypted messages to other ships and bases on shore. It was war without the shooting.

HMCS *Gatineau* at sea.

Those two destroyers were the last ships Harry served on. In 1965 he was sent to Washington, attached to the Canadian embassy. He has never spoken of his work there, but it was almost certainly naval intelligence, shared with Canada's NATO allies, in particular, the United States. The Naval List cryptically classifies Harry as a Code 09, which was communications.

"He would have been on the staff of the embassy there," says Ted Kelly. "We had a defence liaison officer in Washington, so there would have been an attaché there. Harry would have been on the embassy staff, probably with the responsibility for maintaining the relationships with the communications people in the United States Navy. He also would have been involved in monitoring technological equipment developments because of the nature of that industry in the United States, which was well in advance of our own."

Harry's last posting in the navy was in Gander, where he was commander of the base. In many ways, it was coming home. As the helicopter flies, Gander is only seventy-one kilometres from Musgrave Harbour.

The Cold War was still on; Gander, because of its unique position, jutting out from North America far into the North Atlantic, was a vital listening post, in particular for submarine traffic in the North Atlantic. You can't pry a word out of Harry on the subject of what went on there. All he will say is that, like in his postings on the various ships, he was "reading other people's mail."

"When he came to Gander, he was the commander, and they were setting up what, for lack of a better term, was a listening station, which the locals affectionately called the turkey farm. The locals in Gander called soldiers turkeys at the time, I don't know if they still do," says John Steele.

"As you flew into Gander you could see the turkey farm. It was a circular enclosure — a square building within a circular enclosure having high antennas and wires and all that type of stuff." Civilians, even those working at the airport, could only guess what all that equipment was for.

When lieutenant-commander Steele arrived in Gander, he brought his own form of military discipline and his own likes and dislikes. One thing he did not like was smoking, even the smell of smoke. "When Dad took up his posting in Gander, the commander of the base was given a car and a driver," says Peter Steele. "His first day he went up to the base in his finest navy blues, all pressed. I even remember the car, a black Plymouth, and as Dad went out to his first day the driver was smoking. Dad sent him off to go and clean the car right away. Let me say that he expressed his displeasure and the driver understood that he was never to smoke in the car again."

Harry was base commander in Gander from 1969 to 1974, the longest stretch in one posting in his thirty-year career in the navy. Since neither Harry nor anyone who served with him will say much about what went on there at the time, we can only surmise by looking back what events took place in those years. The United States was embroiled in the Vietnam War and would not leave until 1973.

In August of 1968, the Soviet Union invaded Czechoslovakia, crushing a liberalization movement there, and exerting its hold on the so-called Eastern bloc for the next twenty years. Tensions between the Soviets and NATO continued in the North Atlantic and in the air. Soviet planes would test how close they could come to Canadian and American airspace, while their surface vessels and submarines played tag with American and Canadian warships.

All of this meant radio traffic, and monitoring it and deciphering it was the job overseen by lieutenant-commander Harry Steele, a naval man who was commanding an airbase. But the turkey farm was more important than the airbase at the height of the Cold War. Goose Bay was where the fighter jocks trained and the Italians flew their planes upside down over the runway. "Gander was [more of] a communications establishment. A lot of that was radio supplementary as they called the listening posts," says Ted Kelly. Gander was about intelligence and The Commander was the expert.

There was a branch of the navy called Radio Special. They had stations at sea and on land, in the Haida Gwaii [the Queen Charlotte Islands, as they were then called] off the coast of British Columbia, across the North, and one of the biggest, if not the largest, was at Gander. The home base was Ottawa. We can forget the past tense; these operations still go on, perhaps almost as much today as they did during the Cold War.

Not only did these bases listen for radio traffic, they also used direction-finding techniques to figure out which ships were where. If NATO intelligence services wanted a piece of information, key bases such as Gander would help find that out. Electronic spycraft. Highly secret stuff.

"It was fundamentally a communications station. There was a radar base there. The base was all-encompassing; we had what they called an air weapons control, which was run by the air force. We had a search-and-rescue component at the base that I was serving on, which, at that time, was an old base and very small — it's much bigger today. It was a direction-finding station and Harry came there as the commanding officer of the whole thing. The air force and the coast guard came under him," says Reid Nicholson, a naval officer who served with Harry at Gander for five years.

When asked if he ever found or listened to anything interesting, he has a curt response: "No, but if I did I wouldn't talk about it. A long time ago be damned; it makes no difference to me. I can't go into that, and I'm not trying to be coy, I just can't."

As Harry's sons point out, his career in the navy was not something their father spoke about at home. "That part of our father's life he kept very much to himself. He never shared with us about the ships that he went on or about what he did with the communications or being trained by the Brits," says Peter Steele. "We were very young at the time, and as we came up and we'd ask him about that it was either one-liners or, if pushed on it, it was obtuse responses that were very vacuous without much content or substance to them.

"I remember he spent a lot of time in Tampa, which … was a large U.S. military facility. He'd go down there every year we were posted in Washington for the better part of a month, and he would never tell us about what he was working on or what he did, and to this day he never has. So, he was a guy who lived by a code: the Official Secrets Act."

The Cold War is over but the Cold War warriors are going to the grave with their secrets.

Following his stint as commander of the base at Gander, Harry retired from the Royal Canadian Navy. Over the years, Harry has stated that he left the navy because of the government's decision to integrate the different services. Reid says he agrees totally with Harry's position on the integration of the armed forces and the new uniforms. "Harry resisted putting on the green uniform. When they brought this in, a lot of us had a really strong opinion. This, to us, was an absolutely incredible insult and was asinine from the very beginning and doomed to fail, which is why, as history proved, they moved back to the old uniforms, as far as they can.

"As I recall it, I don't know if he ever did put on a green uniform, and if he did it was done under duress. He was a lieutenant-commander. He was never a major (the equivalent rank, though the Naval List disputes that claim). There was a group of us, who I will call navy people, who maintained their naval ranks, such as chief petty officers. There was an admiral, who I don't remember by name, who sent a message around saying he didn't care what anybody else said, he wouldn't serve under this and there were a lot of people who shared that view."

Bill Shead has more than one theory about why Harry left the navy, and he believes that there was more to it than just unification and the green uniform. An important reason for Harry leaving, he believes, was that promotion was slow in the navy, and getting slower as the Trudeau government spent less on defence. Fewer ships meant fewer opportunities for command.

"Career opportunities for naval officers began to shrink in the 1960s: we got rid of the aircraft carrier, and our ships were downsizing. We were paying off the old Second World War vessels, and the new ships were coming online, but they weren't coming along as fast as we were paying off the older ships. So opportunities for command and for further progression kept contracting. I would think that Harry, having ambitions and having knowledge of what was going on in the outside world, saw a tremendous opportunity that he wanted to seize on civvy street. He had studied what was going on in the finance world, and he was not a fellow who would want to miss a real opportunity to do something. One of the things about being a communicator, he saw things coming in technology that some of us in other specialties probably did not see. I know of one petty officer second-class on the ship who was a communicator [and] who got out at about the same time as Harry, and he bought into cable and did extremely well for himself."

His family members think Harry should have been promoted beyond the rank of lieutenant-commander. Harry might think so, too, but he is too modest to say that so many years later.

"I might have been, but that's the natural thinking to have. You always [think] you [are] more deserving. But I'll tell you one thing they did do that shocked the hell out of everybody: you had to wait eight years to be promoted from lieutenant to lieutenant-commander. It was automatic. So, they took six people to promote after six and a half years, and I was one of the ones they picked in all the navy, so I was pleased with that. It was the best victory I ever had in my life. So, I have no bitter feelings at all about the navy," says Harry.

Leaving the question of whether or not Harry was worthy of further promotion aside, it is clear that all who knew Harry had the greatest respect for him. Commenting on Harry as a naval officer, Reid Nicholson says, "Harry Steele represented almost everything in my mind that I believed a naval officer should represent. He didn't suffer fools lightly. I'm a great believer that rank is not a reward but a challenge, and you have a responsibility to the people above you to do the job and to the people below you. Naval leadership is unlike in the army, where they say, 'You go here and you go there.' Naval leadership is all about 'Follow me' and there's a difference in that. That was Harry Steele: 'This is what I want you to do and this is how we're going to do it' … it was sort of a 'we.' I had the greatest respect for him."

The navy experience prepared Harry Steele for his future success in business, success that did not surprise Captain Ted Kelly. "I wasn't surprised at all. I'll give you a quick anecdote: in about 1964 or so, the 5th Squadron paid a visit to Philadelphia in support of a trade exhibition show. External Affairs put on these trade exhibitions to drum up interest in things. I guess we were about four or five ships then went into Philadelphia. The External Affairs people were having difficulty coping with this particular trade show, and it was either the trade consul or the ambassador who mentioned something at a luncheon, either on the first day or just before the show opened, to the squadron commander. He came to Harry and said, 'Harry, they tell me they're having trouble down there, would you go down there and sort them out?'

"Harry went down, and he found out that a lot of the difficulties were communications difficulties — queries that were coming from different organizations and people — it was just kind of a chaotic situation. Harry gathered up a bunch of communications people from the ships and took them down. This was a four- or five-day exposition and pretty soon Harry was running it. The

External Affairs people just weren't up to the take-charge thing, and Harry just stepped in and took charge of it. At the end of it, the ambassador was effusive in his remarks about how the navy had saved the day for them, principally Harry.

"I used to bump into Harry at the airport or something after he had left the navy and was involved with Eastern Provincial Airways. He was certainly industrious. Harry was a hard-working guy, and he was hands on. You could see it then, and you could see it when he owned the airline. He had a good relationship with all the people that worked for him. Even recently, to give you some sense, as you know the Steele Group have a lot of automobile dealerships here and in Halifax, which is the business of his son Rob. I was buying a car a couple of years ago, and I went into one of the Steele dealerships and I was chatting, asking how long had they been there and did they know the Steele family, etc., and I asked if they were closely involved in the business and they said, 'Well, we always see Harry.' It wasn't really Harry's thing, as he was involved in other aspects of it, but they all knew him because he would go around and make a point of ensuring that he knew who they were. That was Harry. He was a very down-to-earth guy, a great raconteur who always had a good story for you when he met you."

Harry's time in the navy formed his attitudes toward business. He could solve a problem in a hurry. On a warship, if there was something wrong, it had to be fixed, no excuses.

"One thing I learned from my training in the Royal Navy was to believe fervently that anything was possible. I believed that, and I still do," says Harry.

One aspect of his advanced training, which he was not that keen on, involved learning to fly — or at least coming to understand the world of pilots. "We had to take compulsory pilot training, and I had absolutely no desire ever to be a pilot. None. Zero. I remember flying in an aircraft in the U.K., and I told the instructor, 'I don't want to fly airplanes,' and he told me if I didn't want to fly airplanes let's fly bottom up and he rolled the airplane over," remembers Harry.

In retrospect, the lesson was that if a naval officer was going to command people, he better understand everything that is happening on his watch, and that includes military aircraft. "It was a valuable lesson," says Harry, and something that guided him when he was running a complex business empire later in life. He always wanted to know what the people working for him were doing.

The navy was the making of Harry Steele. It is doubtful he would have had such opportunity if he had stayed on the lower layers of society. Tough to say, but true.

"The navy gave him a lot," says Peter Steele. "It gave him discipline and it helped him understand how to develop structure, how to put a plan together and how to make things happen. It taught him self-discipline, how to be on time, and it also opened him up to what could be by seeing Africa and spending time in Europe and going to these places."

Sitting in the restaurant of The Albatross in the fall of 2017, Harry agrees with that sentiment.

"The navy trained you well," says Harry. "You knew how to do things and you were never scared to do things; you always had a certain amount of independence, which is important." That self-confidence carried over to the next stage of his life as a businessman.

Commander Steele Retires

Over four years ago, a new base commander arrived at CFS *Gander*. Commander Harry Steele, who is himself a native Newfoundlander, took control of CFS *Gander* just as the dawn of a new era in military communications was about to begin. Prior to that, people jokingly referred to the Canadian military presence in Gander as being a taxpayer's dilemma, as there was little military significance to justify the continuation of CFS *Gander*'s operations.

However, times have changed, and the feelings of apathy and pessimism that were present amongst the military personnel stationed here five or six years ago has long gone. No small part of this improved picture can be attributed to Commander Steele, as it was he who tackled the task of upgrading the base's operations, its significance, and, as well, did a darn good job of making the personnel stationed here just a little bit prouder of the fact they were associated with CFS *Gander*. Ample proof of this was the massive increase in the number of personnel who put in for extensions of their stay here in the last several years.

Relations between the civilian and military sections of Gander's population have also become warmer in the four and a half years that Commander Steele has been running the show. Oh yes, there has been the odd reversal, caused by trivial differences of opinion over such things as taxes; however, the meaningful community-military rapport that Commander Steele engineered was more than strong enough to weather such petty factors.

On Friday morning, Commander Steele officially turns over the control of CFS *Gander* to a new commanding officer and in the process he will be honored by those he has served since arriving here. Yet Gander also has something to be thankful for as Commander Steele has selected to make his home here. Gander should be proud of the fact that we will be able to boast of having men of the stature of Harry Steele dwelling among us. This individual's drive and organizational ability has helped us to build quite a reputation not only for himself but also for Gander as well.

Welcome, Mr. Steele, to the civilian world of Gander, and here's hoping your energies and ambitions will remain with you for years to come. If so, Gander stands to have an able servant in her midst.

Records from the Naval List

Year	Where Serving	Name Rank Seniority
1952–1953	Cabot	Acting sub-lieutenant, Royal Canadian Navy
1954	Ontario	Acting sub-lieutenant, Royal Canadian Navy
1954–1955	Magnificent	Acting sub-lieutenant, Royal Canadian Navy
1955–1956	Mercury	Acting sub-lieutenant, Royal Canadian Navy
1956–1958	Nootka	Sub-lieutenant, Royal Canadian Navy
1958	Sault Ste. Marie	Lieutenant, Royal Canadian Navy
1959	Stadacona	Lieutenant, Royal Canadian Navy
1960	Cornwallis	Lieutenant, Royal Canadian Navy
1961	Fort Erie	Lieutenant, Royal Canadian Navy
1962	Gatineau	Lieutenant, Royal Canadian Navy
1963	Gatineau	Lieutenant-commander, Royal Canadian Navy
1964	Restigouche	Lieutenant-commander, Royal Canadian Navy
1965	Joint Maritime Warfare School	Lieutenant-commander (Code 09: Communications), Royal Canadian Navy
1969	Washington	Major, Royal Canadian Navy

Four

Family Life

*My father looked upon people who wanted
to golf or sail with great disdain.*
— John Steele

Catherine Steele said she would never marry a man who went
to sea. By that, she probably meant someone like her illustrious father, Captain Arch Thornhill, the skipper of schooners and
trawlers. Instead, she married a man who spent long stretches at
sea, but aboard frigates, destroyers, and aircraft carriers.

When Harry and Catherine returned to Canada after his stint
in England, they started a family: Peter was born in September of
1957, Rob in June of 1961, and John in December of 1965. The
Steele family moved around, but not as much as some military
families. While Harry was at sea, the years from 1953 to 1965,
the family home was in Dartmouth, Nova Scotia.

When Harry was stationed in Washington and Gander, he
could live a normal family life. One thing that *was* different
was that Harry shared almost nothing of his work life with his
family. While many fathers and husbands would come home
with tales of what went on in the office, Harry kept that part
of his life separate.

"In terms of the military stuff, no, he didn't talk about that at
home," says John. Though once he was out of the navy, it was

Catherine and Harry on their wedding day.

The wedding party. To the bride and groom's right: Best Man, Lieutenant Cyril Kirby; Maid of Honour, Miss Mary Williams; Bridesmaids, Miss Shirley Pope and Miss Shirley Parsons. In front: Flower Girl, Sherril Trask, and Ring Bearer, Gary Maunder. Not pictured: Ushers, Sub-Lieutenants Malcolm Drover and Thomas Cahill.

a different story. "In terms of business, yes, he would talk about that. He totally lived it, and it was always discussed within our home. As a young fellow, I remember Dad taking me to meetings and having business discussions with people and I'd just be sitting there taking it all in. Some people found it a bit awkward that this seven-, eight-, or ten-year-old kid was sitting there while they were discussing various business issues."

"Home life, wherever we were, whether it was 6507 Divine Street or whether it was Gander or Dartmouth, it was very normal. We lived at the time in Forces' PMQs, which is armed forces housing — [this housing was] not necessarily on the base but [it was] armed forces housing. I remember when we first lived in Gander, when Dad took up his posting, we lived at 25 Boyd Street, which was an armed forces house, and, as CO, you stayed in an armed forces house," says Peter.

As well as a navy man, Harry was a family man. The Steeles lived at 6507 Divine Street in McLean, Virginia, a suburb of Washington, D.C. Though he would travel a bit, in particular to a naval base in Tampa, Florida, Harry had a desk job, so he spent a lot of time with his wife, Catherine, and their young family.

"Wherever we lived, life was very normal, very middle class. You raise your family and hopefully impart on them the skills and the education so that they can go out and make the most of what they were born with. The same philosophy as so many middle-class Canadians of that generation," says Peter. It was so normal that he recalls that his father was an assistant coach on Peter's Little League baseball team when they lived in Washington.

One of the highlights of navy life for the Steele family was Harry's posting to the embassy in Washington. It was a time of civil unrest in the United States, and Harry wanted to make sure his children, in particular his oldest son, Peter, knew what was happening. In the spring of 1968, both the civil rights icon Martin Luther King Jr. and Robert Kennedy were assassinated. There were marches on Washington, and Harry Steele took his sons to see some of the drama that was unfolding.

"We lived in Washington and Dad was attached to the Canadian embassy. Black people had come from all over the United States under the direction and at the request of the Reverend Ralph Abernathy. It was called Resurrection City. They built shacks all around the White House and all down around Washington, D.C.," says Peter.

The demonstrators occupied the mall in Washington for forty-two days.

"My father took me to that. He would always take my younger brothers and me down to things like that. He tried to impart to us that we're part of a bigger world, and there's a place in it for us, and that the more you are exposed to things, the more capable and able you are going to be."

Catherine and her boys, Rob, John, and Peter.

There were other highlights of living in Washington as the son of a diplomat.

"I remember being at the White House with my mother and father and my brothers when Trudeau was down there (visiting) Nixon. I remember being down there at the assassination of Martin Luther King Jr. and the National Guard cordoning off our neighbourhood," says Peter. "I was playing Little League baseball at the time, and the riots were so crazy that one of the things that got looted were our team shirts."

Peter's younger brother Rob also enjoyed life in Washington. "That was such a glorious time in our lives. I remember when we lived at 36 Richards Drive in Dartmouth, Nova Scotia. I was four years old and my parents had two Volkswagens, a blue one and a white one, and I remember my mother telling my brother Pete and I (John wasn't born then) that we were going to be moving to the United States and I was really excited about moving — why, I don't know. Pete would have been seven or eight years old at the time, and I remember I drove down with my mother and Pete drove down with my father in the VW Bug. We drove in those Beetles to McLean, Virginia, to a house on Divine Street that they were renting. I remember the neighbourhood. I was a four-year-old kid, and we lived there for four years, and I have very strong memories of those years.

"I remember my father — he would have been in his thirties at the time — going off to work in the mornings in his uniform, and we used to go camping, and it was just a fun time. There were a lot of kids in and around the neighbourhood. The Vietnam War was on at the time, and I remember brothers of friends of mine who were over at war in Vietnam and I remember thinking how scary that must have been even as a young kid. That's where I started school as well."

As an adult, Rob has a strong connection to the United States. He has a house in Austin, Texas, the house once owned by the great rock singer Janis Joplin. Rob agrees that the time spent in Washington left him with a positive feeling about the United States.

Harry's public persona is that of a tough businessman who never caves. One might think this stern exterior translated into a man who was a tyrant at home. Nothing could be further from the truth.

"With me, he wasn't a disciplinarian at all. A lot of people are very surprised when I tell them that because the public image of him is one of being stern and a hard taskmaster," says John. "But in terms of me, he wasn't at all; it was my mother who did that with us, with me anyway. If you did something and you got busted for it, you'd rather deal with Dad on it because he might yell and bluster and stuff but he would always relent, but Mum would punish us."

Even if Harry could be relatively easy at home, his business tough-ness did occasionally have an effect on the family. The strike at Eastern Provincial Airways — more on this later — did take its toll. The family was living in Gander at the time, and the workers and their families were their neighbours. So, the boys, who were in school at the time, were forced to spend their days with the sons and daughters of the workers. John says it didn't affect him. But Peter says he noticed it.

"There was a lot of collateral damage, and you asked if it affected me directly and I would say this: If you are of a family of means in a small town you are always conscious of a distinction between you and the rest of the community. The strike really accentuated that distinction. That is my personal takeaway," says Peter.

Five

Stock Market Investor

*It is more important to know when to sell
than when to buy.*

— Harry Steele

Years before he left the navy, Harry Steele became a successful stock market investor, helped at first by his wife Catherine's brother, Roland Thornhill. Roland was a stockbroker in Halifax, working for a small Saint John, New Brunswick, firm called Eastern Securities. Harry opened an account there and started buying small amounts of stock with money left over from his pay in the navy, which was not an extravagant sum.

"Harry became fascinated with the investment business. He used to take me down on board the ship, as he was still in the navy, and I would visit with him and some of his mates in the boardroom. They were all interested in the stock market, but Harry was just obsessed with it," recalls Roland.

Bill Shead recalls that Harry had a good feel for what was going on in the market, and Bill credits Harry with giving him a grounding in the world of money, which paid off down the road, making his retirement that much more comfortable.

"Harry's brother-in-law was involved in the investment field, and he and Harry would often talk finance when they were together having a drink or on a ship," recalls Bill. "We got involved as well, and we learned quite a bit from him. I got interested in it, and I think I started my first investment when I was on that ship and thanks to that I've done fairly well but not in the class of Harry.

"I would think Harry had a sizeable nest egg when he left the navy, which allowed him to go off and into business. He was generous, and he didn't splurge on things, so he was careful. He was conscious that there was a way to make a dollar. Any investment that he made, I'm sure he was aware had some downside potential but a hell of a lot of upside potential. He was not afraid to take a risk."

Even his brother-in-law was surprised at how he took to the market. "I'll tell you how good Harry was: One time when he was just about ready to get out of the navy, he talked to me about becoming a sub-agent for Richardson [Investments, which had acquired Eastern Securities] in Newfoundland. I told him that before becoming an agent, you had to write a test, which would tell them if they had a suitable candidate. So he said he wanted to take it and he came and we put him in a little office there for exactly one hour. I gave him the test and sent it off to Winnipeg where they analyzed it."

The test measured Harry's interest in and knowledge of markets, his ability to pick promising investments, and other qualities that would make him suitable to work in the field. Remember, this was a man who was still in the navy with a full-time job running a complex base in Gander, Newfoundland.

Roland was shocked at the result. "The chap who was in charge in Winnipeg [would] normally review it and comment that the candidate wasn't suitable or was adaptable, and I should pursue it, but in this particular case he called me and said I should hang on to this guy because this was one of the best results they had ever seen."

Harry did not become a sub-agent, but he started to trade heavily. To handle his deals, he dealt, in particular, with two men who would have a profound influence on his business and investing life: the late Nigel Martin, then a Toronto stockbroker, and

Seymour Schulich, whose investment savvy made him one of the richest men in Canada, something that has allowed him to become a generous philanthropist.

Seymour started as a research analyst in the Montreal office of Eastern Securities. At the time, there were not many Jews in the investment business, but that was about to change. Seymour, the city kid from the Snowdon district in Montreal, hit it off with Harry, the kid from Musgrave Harbour. Both had overcome adversity to achieve success, and the two became lifelong friends. For a while, Seymour was chairman of Newfoundland Capital Corporation, and in later years the two men and their wives went on cruises together.

"Seymour has got an ego the size of Manhattan, but there's no better friend in the world," says Harry.

One of Seymour's closest friends was Nigel Martin, a Toronto broker originally from Montreal. Martin was a boy wonder as a stock trader, and after working for a large firm, he became a partner at Thomson Kernaghan (a stockbrokerage), with a 15 percent stake. Harry was a client at the firm through his connection with Seymour Schulich. One of the brokers he dealt with there was David Bruce, an affable Scot who continues to work as a broker to this day.

"I met Harry through Nigel. When we left Dominion Securities [DS] in 1973, Nigel and I went to join Ted Kernaghan, and we were at Kernaghan … then. Nigel's association with Seymour Schulich was from his Montreal days when he was at DS and Seymour was a good friend of Harry's. When Harry asked Seymour for a broker, he mentioned Nigel's name. So he called Nigel in 1974, and we started from there, forty-three years ago," says David.

At the time, Harry was still the base commander of Gander, but, as mentioned, he was already a successful stock market investor with a sizeable portfolio. As Roland Thornhill notes, Harry had a natural feel for markets, and he studied the way markets move and how to value a particular stock by reading about it.

One company that came into his sights was Eastern Provincial Airways. The company was based in Gander and, as we will learn

Boeing 737 in EPA livery.

later, Harry was interested in attracting its employees to The Albatross, the hotel he and his wife owned in Gander. He could see that the shares of EPA were pretty beaten up and he put in an order with Nigel Martin and David Bruce to keep an eye on the company's stock.

Eastern Provincial was not the only stock Harry was interested in. It was different from the others he traded, however, because he was not interested in acquiring control, or at least a sizeable position, of any other firm. Harry was a trader, and David Bruce says he was a very disciplined trader.

"He was very successful building up his nest egg; he was an excellent trader. He was impatient; he wanted the stock right then, 'Right now' he would say. Any time Harry had a profit, he'd say, 'Let's go, let's leave some for somebody else.' He was not someone who would ride things forever."

Bruce estimates that by the time Harry left the navy his fortune was close to a million dollars — a lot of money then. That is a figure that other people outside the family have also come up with.

Bruce remembers the price Harry was paying for Eastern Provincial stock more than forty years ago. "We were buying the stock for between two and three dollars, but I don't know … the precise deal he did with the Crosbies." Details of that transaction are dealt with in chapter 7.

As a Scotsman, David Bruce loved to fish for Atlantic salmon, the same fish that rises to the fly in Harry's fishing camps in Labrador and swims in the lochs and rivers of the highlands of Scotland. David Bruce and Seymour Schulich were the perfect guests at Harry's fishing camp. When they were on the river or over drinks and dinner, the conversation was all about business and especially the stock market. Just the way Harry liked it.

"Harry Steele was a spectacular guy, someone who would always give you the time of day. He knew everybody by their first name and where they came from and what they were all about. He had guys who would follow him to the ends of the earth. He was an absolute guy's guy," says David.

"He was very easy to talk to and not tough at all unless things weren't going his way. I've seen him angry probably twice since I've known him. One of them was when he had the big pilot's strike at EPA; he was absolutely furious at his pilots."

Though Harry Steele's stock market acumen helped him in business, some of his family members and colleagues say at times it was a distraction, if not an obsession. If Harry had one vice, it was the stock market. A man who relied on information, whether it was a Soviet radio transmission or a stock tip from his network, Harry was always on the lookout for a winner.

"That was Harry's only addiction, to use your word, but it never killed him, so what the hell," says one of his closest advisers.

Six

Seymour Schulich

Seymour has got an ego the size of Manhattan but there's no better friend in the world.

— Harry Steele

Harry Steele's face lights up when he talks about Seymour Schulich. Peter Steele says Seymour is one of his father's true close friends. "My father has never had a lot of friends; he had a lot of acquaintances. He was a very private man," says Peter.

As noted, Harry met Seymour pretty much at the start of Schulich's career as an analyst, when he was with Eastern Securities. It was an era when the financial business was not that open to Jews. Eastern didn't care, and neither did Harry.

"Seymour was at Eastern Securities, which was the only firm that would hire him at the time because he was Jewish. He was the analyst, and that's how he met Harry, through Rolly," says David Bruce.

Schulich grew up in Notre-Dame-de-Grâce, an inner suburb of Montreal. It was far away culturally from life in Musgrave Harbour, so some would think that Harry and Seymour would have had little in common. Although their backgrounds are certainly different, the two are, in fact, much alike. What the two have in common is intelligence, a work ethic that would put just about anyone to shame, and an ambition to succeed.

"They are very different type guys in a lot of ways, [but Schulich's] intelligence and success commanded the respect of my father, and I think [Seymour] appreciated and respected how my father could interact with people and how, when he came in a room, the dynamics of the room changed," says John Steele.

When Harry took over Eastern Provincial Airways, Seymour became a key adviser and was non-executive chairman of EPA from 1980 to 1986.

"Seymour was important for Harry businesswise. He gave him a lot of advice. Seymour was chairman of Newfoundland Capital at one time. So I think he was quite important in the leadership of the business direction it took," says David Bruce.

When it came time to sell EPA, Seymour was in favour, since in his view airlines are too capital intensive: in plain English, airlines drain cash — they have expensive staff and money is always needed to buy new aircraft. There are also many unpredictable things that affect the bottom line, such as rising fuel costs and passenger loads. And there is always the possibility of strikes.

Radio stations are the opposite. "I guess it might have been my idea to get into radio," says Seymour. He reasoned that radio stations did not take a lot of money to operate, unlike the other businesses Harry was in, such as airlines and transportation. Radio stations remain a great place for advertisers in cities, but they are especially valuable in smaller markets. John Steele, who was involved in the radio business, agrees. "There's no doubt that Seymour turned him on to radio," says John.

Schulich definitely provided Harry important investing advice, but according to John Steele, he never got involved in running Harry's businesses. "He was close to my father in terms of stock market stuff for sure, but in terms of operational things … after a while, my father was on his own."

According to Peter Steele, "Seymour Schulich, from the days of being a broker, opened my father's inquisitiveness about the capital markets and that whole world, which ignited a lifelong passion in him for the stock market. In terms of the success in business that my father had, Seymour was instrumental in introducing him to the accessing of finance through the capital markets and guiding him and navigating him in the early days through that process. That is Seymour on the business side of it. And we'll just say that they were personal friends too."

Harry was opinionated about politics, and he and Seymour would share their opinions, which were on the same wavelength. Schulich thought Harry would have done well in politics.

"Over the years I met a lot of provincial leaders. Harry would have been better than all of them," says Seymour, sitting in his relatively modest offices in midtown Toronto. "In some ways, it's a tragedy. Harry could have been premier of Newfoundland when he was around sixty years old. I tried to get him to go, but among other things, he was uncomfortable with public speaking."

Seymour points out that there is one section of the population with whom Harry is particularly popular: women. It is not because he is a matinee idol, but because he is an old-fashioned gentleman. "My wife loves Harry. Women like Harry because he is non-threatening, a father figure. That's why he would have been elected premier of Newfoundland if he had run," says Seymour. "On top of that, Harry is a people guy."

Difficult to explain what makes a friendship tick. These two men did more than chat on the phone and meet at board meetings. In later life, they went on cruises together. "We went on nine cruises with our wives," says Seymour. He also has a great deal of admiration for Catherine Steele and endowed a music chair in her name at McGill University in Montreal.

When Harry's health started to fail, Seymour showed real compassion.

"A short time ago I had a call from him, and we chatted for a while. It was a very emotional call for him, asking about my father," says John.

At the end of a two-hour conversation with Seymour Schulich, his personality changed from the gruff businessman he was at the start to friendly confidante; certainly the person Harry came to know. He let down his guard, the protection many rich men wear as a kind of shield to protect themselves from sycophants and predators, and spoke of his feelings for his longtime friend.

"Harry Steele is one of the finest human beings I have ever known. I love him."

Seymour Schulich's 1998 autobiography, *Life and Business Lessons*, includes this section on Harry Steele:

Friends

Real relationships are built up over twenty-, thirty-, and forty-year time periods. My wise, street-smart father told me I would be very lucky to have two close friends in my lifetime outside my family. His rule for defining a friend is someone who would loan you $10,000 (that's about $100,000 in today's dollars). From the perspective of age sixty-six, I realize Dad was right. At this stage, I don't have the years left to form really close friendships.

Partners share a common interest when they're building something together. They always command a very special place in one's hearts and thoughts. Ex-partners often move on to new ventures with their families, especially if sons are involved.

Usually, mavens (see *The Tipping Point* by Malcolm Gladwell) make close friends with connectors or salesmen. That has been the case in my life.

One friendship that lasted forty years featured a man who had very unique attributes worth examining. Let's keep his anonymity by calling him Harry. Now, Harry came up through the military, retired at forty-two years old after attaining a high rank and serving several years in Canadian Intelligence in Washington. Everybody, male and female, liked this man. Why?

Harry made a lot of his contacts by inviting people to fishing camps in Newfoundland and Labrador. He and a rather colourful Newfoundland best friend entertained countless businessmen, premiers, prime ministers, and U.S. presidents at these camps. There's no better way to learn about people than spending three days trapped in a fishing camp with them. This setting sifts out the alcoholics, the frivolous, the smart, the dumb, and generally exposes most personality flaws and attributes.

Harry showed all his guests great respect. Each one was made to feel he or she was important. When Harry spoke to a person, his eyes didn't dart around the room seeking more important folks to buttonhole. The person he was talking to was the centre of his world (at that moment). He never talked about himself or his family. He always talked about the other person, his or her interests, views, business, and what investments he or she thought might possess some merit.

Although a very successful businessman, he lived fairly simply. (His only toys were a thirteen-year-old Ferrari and a maroon fedora). At his fishing camps, he was the leader and puppet master. He maneuvered people around without their knowing it. He never bragged, was an excellent host, and engendered great respect from virtually all the staff and employees.

We often went on cruise ships together. He and his wife used tea time to get to know a lot of fellow travellers. I considered that to be a waste of time. Not deterred, every day he trolled the tea lounge and invariably knew all the key players on board.

The fascinating thing about Harry was how he could bond with people in a short period of time. He probably never read Dale Carnegie, yet used all the techniques in the book *How to Win Friends and Influence People*. I've never met a man respected and beloved by more people. I'm still trying to analyze how he does it.

Seven

Eastern Provincial Airways

Nobody has ever made any money on a sustained basis in Canada operating an airline.

— Harry Steele

Despite Harry Steele's claim that it is impossible to make money operating an airline in Canada, he made a success of Eastern Provincial Airways, the business that was the start of his business career and the making of his fortune. Harry never thought of actually owning the airline until after he left the navy, but that's just what he ended up doing.

Eastern Provincial Airways

Harry Steele knew the history of Eastern Provincial Airways long before he got involved with the airline. It was a legend in Newfoundland, flying into every region of the island and Labrador, bringing in supplies to remote mining camps, landing fishermen on lakes and salmon streams, and evacuating the sick and injured to hospitals.

Eastern Provincial Airways was the fourth largest airline in Canada in 1978 but it was dwarfed by Air Canada and CP Air. Number three was a regional airline in western Canada. EPA had 850 employees when Harry Steele took it over.

The airline was started in 1949, the same year Newfoundland joined Confederation. Chesley A. Crosbie (father of John Crosbie, the federal politician and Tory cabinet minister) bought the operation from Eric Blackwood, a pilot with the Royal Canadian Air Force in the Second World War. Among the first aircraft was a Cessna T-50, a converted twin-engine military transport from the war. It carried four passengers and had a range of 1,200 kilometres or 750 miles. Blackwood registered the name Eastern Provincial Airways, but the financial backer was Chesley Crosbie.

From the start, the fledgling airline operated from Gander, a combination military/civilian airfield with runways capable of handling any traffic.

"It was started on a shoestring budget, with a couple of small airplanes and hopes for a bright future by Newfoundland businessman Ches Crosbie and his managing director and pilot, Eric Blackwood. Marsh Jones was its first full-time pilot," wrote Harry in his introduction to Marsh Jones's 1998 book on the early history of the airline: *The Little Airline That Could. Eastern Provincial Airways. The First Fifteen Years.*

Harry's introduction continues: "Those were the days of seat-of-the-pants flying with little more than a map, compass and radio to enable pilots of the fledgling airline to carry out their assigned duties. Flying conditions were often harsh and unforgiving; landing sites were largely untested, and much was left to the pilot's judgment and initiative. But the little airline survived, and grew."

Royal Cooper was the chief pilot for Eastern Provincial starting in 1956. He, too, wrote a book: *Tales from a Pilot's Logbook.* It is a fascinating look at his life as a pilot; he logged more than twenty thousand hours in the air on sixty different types of aircraft. Some of the most interesting sections deal with his time as a bush pilot for EPA.

The native of Summerville, Bonavista Bay, flew with a Newfoundland squadron in England in the Second World War.

Harry's first business success — EPA: The Little Airline That Could.

Royal flew the Mosquito, a twin-engine fighter-bomber, one of the fastest aircraft of the war.

When he returned to Canada, Royal had a hard time finding work as a pilot. There was a glut of wartime pilots also looking for work. Eventually, he started work for Maritime Central Airways, then in 1954, he was hired by Ches Crosbie for EPA. He moved to Gander, where he lived for the rest of his life, serving on the town council for thirteen years, and three terms as mayor.

EPA bought its second Beaver from de Havilland in Toronto. The single-engine, short-take-off-and-landing plane was designed and built in Canada for Canadian conditions. Equipped with skis or amphibious floats (floats with retractable wheels), the plane could be used anywhere.

There are stories of brave pilots flying in all kinds of weather. Royal and his team could do repairs on the spot to get stricken aircraft flying out of remote lakes. One time they had to stuff a damaged float with inner tubes so it could hold up until they got the plane into the air.

On one medical evacuation, Royal remembers the water was choppy, and the patient had an injured back. He said he screamed every time the plane hit a wave. Once the plane was airborne, the man's pain subsided and the man, who had obviously not lost his sense of humour, quipped: "I think next time I'll walk."

Royal started the airline's service to Greenland, perhaps the most unusual thing the airline ever did. In 1958 the Danish government hired EPA to connect with SAS, the Scandinavian airline, from the main airport to small communities up and down the coast of Greenland. The principal aircraft used were the Canso, a fairly large amphibious aircraft that was a leftover from the war, along with de Havilland Otters, the larger version of the Beaver.

"To me, the hardest part of flying in Greenland was learning to pronounce the place names. However, we were soon rolling such names as Ivigtut [now Ivittuut], Qutdligssat [now Qullissat], Sukkertoppen, Julianehab [now Qaqortoq], and Egedesminde [now Aasiaat] off our tongues as if we had lived there all our lives," says Royal, who retired in 1972, long before Harry took control of the airline.

In 1963 Eastern Provincial merged with the much larger Maritime Central Airways, which was founded by two men from the Maritimes, Carl Burke of Prince Edward Island and Josiah Anderson from Moncton, New Brunswick.

One of its first planes was a Boeing 247. That is not a typo. The 247 was a small twin-engine aircraft, advanced for its day when it first started flying in the 1930s. It was able to carry ten passengers and had a range of 1,200 kilometres or 750 miles, enough to make it from Halifax to St. John's.

Maritime Central expanded and continued to modernize its fleet with DC3s, DC4s, DC6s, and the British Viscount airliner. When Eastern Provincial took it over it was the third largest airline in Canada. By the time Harry Steele took command in 1979, EPA was flying Boeing 737s, a long way from the Boeing 247.

When Paul Hellyer, Canada's minister of defence, decided to unify the Canadian Armed Forces and scrap naval uniforms, Harry decided to leave the Royal Canadian Navy. As has been mentioned, the unification of the armed forces was not the only reason behind Harry's decision, but it certainly helped him to make that difficult choice. Also making things easier was the fact that Harry was in a very good financial position. Catherine Steele's skill in the real estate market and hotel management provided significant income, and of course Harry had had a good deal of early success in the stock market.

Even when he was in the navy, business began to occupy more and more of Harry's time and interest. Harry Steele had become a student of the market and what made business tick. If he could pick a winner in the stock market, he could find a company to buy and run. The navy served him well, but life in business beckoned.

On leaving the navy, what seemed like a golden opportunity was staring him in the face. Newfoundland's only airline was in trouble, and the Crosbie family, a prominent a name in the St. John's business world back then, were looking for a way to save it or sell it.

Harry Steele was forty-five years old when he quit the navy in 1974. The managers of EPA thought they could use a man with military experience and an outgoing personality. They hired Harry as vice-president of traffic. He lasted less than a year on the job.

A man who was used to things running with military precision thought the airline was terribly run.

"These guys don't know if they are pitching or catching," is one of Harry's favourite sayings and one that applied, in his opinion, to the management of EPA.

"He got in there with those guys trying to get the business for The Albatross, and when he was up there and joined them on the management team in the marketing role, he came to have no respect for them," says his son Peter Steele. "He saw that what had started out as trying to get the business over to The Albatross was an opportunity."

Looking at the airline from the inside, and looking at its depressed stock price, Harry decided to try for control. He already owned a fair chunk of shares of Eastern Provincial Airways.

"Shortly after he left the company he put together the wherewithal to buy the company. I think he was convinced that under new ownership and leadership that something could be made of the airline," says Roy Rideout.

Coming up with the "wherewithal" took a lot of juggling. Harry mortgaged his house and the family stake in The Albatross Hotel and put it all together. It helped that he already had a sizeable slice of EPA stock, purchased at bargain basement prices. Harry was one of the largest shareholders apart from Andrew Crosbie, Chesley's son.

"Business at the hotel started going straight up, making money. So that's how Dad was able to leverage cash out of that and every other asset he had to take over the airline," says Rob Steele.

"There's no doubt about it, acquiring EPA was a turning point because it ramped up the public image for him, and it was Atlantic Canada and beyond at that point," says John Steele. "It catapulted him not only onto the Atlantic Canada stage but the national stage as well. It was a terrible business to be in, very hard to make money, but it was very sexy because it was travel and all that stuff. It certainly was a game-changer."

Harry didn't just drift into the airline. For years he had been an astute student of the stock market. It was only natural that he would take a look at the only publicly traded company that operated out of Gander, Newfoundland. At the time, the airline was losing close to a million dollars a year. Its shares were trading around $1.85. Despite the fact that the firm was losing money and its shares were in the cellar, Harry believed EPA had potential, and so slowly he started to buy into the firm.

"I knew Miller's [EPA president, Keith Miller] or Crosbie's shares were going to be sold, and I knew control was going to be changed and had to change," said Harry over breakfast at The Albatross Hotel in Gander one October morning in 2017. It is more than thirty years since his day-to-day involvement with Eastern Provincial, but every day he still wears the blue tie with red EPA logo with the red stylized bird. He knows how important that first venture was to his future success, and makes a subtle point of announcing it every day.

"Harry had just come from Washington to Gander where he was the base commander," says David Bruce. "At that point, when we met him, he was thinking about buying Eastern Provincial Airways from the Crosbies, and he gave me an order to accumulate EPA stock. For about two years we would buy four hundred one day and seven hundred the next day, and we just kept buying and buying it until he got a reasonable position and then he went in and bid to Crosbie for the rest of it, and he won it."

Harry's son Peter, a man with an amazing memory and in many ways keeper of much family lore, remembers pretty much the same story. "He kept accumulating stock when it was beaten up to get to be the number two position [i.e., the second largest shareholder] and then bought out number one and three. Andrew Crosbie was number one, and number three was the president of the company, Keith Miller," says Peter.

"The original deal for the airline is written on the back of an EPA placemat. That was pretty cool," says John. He knew, even as a young boy, that buying the airline was a gamble. "I knew growing up that everything was in play and everything was at

Harry beside the jet engine of an EPA Boeing 737.

risk, and we were moving along, but I also knew in the back of my mind that this thing could capsize at any minute. They risked everything, and it was just such a crazy business, and it was so dysfunctional a company, and trying to wrestle that to the ground you knew that any time it could go."

While the original deal was scribbled on the back of a place-mat, the formal agreement was done by the lawyers in St. John's. On October 27, 1978, the following letter changed control of Newfoundland's airline from the Crosbie family, top of the heap in the tight-knit world of business in Newfoundland, to Harry Steele, the man who started life in Musgrave Harbour:

Option to Purchase Shares

To: H.R. Steele
Gander, Nfld.

In consideration of other good and valuable con-sideration and the sum of $1.00 now paid to the undersigned by you (receipt of which is hereby acknowledged), the undersigned hereby grants to you an option irrevocable with the time hereinafter limited to purchase the following number of shares owned or controlled by the undersigned in the capital stock of Eastern Provincial Airways Limited being common shares without par value, at the price of $8.00 per share net-net.

Andrew C. Crosbie	214,875
Crosbie & Company	27,900
Newfoundland Engineering & Const. Co.	84,774
Andrew C. Crosbie Lifetime Trust	45,000
TOTAL	372,549

This option is exercisable at any time up to and including the 29st [sic] day of December 1978 by mailing a notice in writing addressed to the undersigned at the address given below or by serving such notice in writing personally and if the option is exercised the undersigned shall sell or cause to be sold, and you or your assignors shall purchase the said shares at the price of $8.00 per share net-net. The said sale shall be closed within seven days of the exercise of the option when payment shall be made by bank drafts or certified cheques upon delivery of share certificates representing the said shares duly endorsed in blank for the transfer.

This option may be exercised by you or your successors or assigns.

Time shall be the essence hereof.

In witness whereof I have signed this 27th day of October 1978.

Andrew C. Crosbie
St. John's, Nfld.

Witness
H. Wareham

That slog of legalese was translated into plain English by the headline in the *Daily News* of St. John's almost a month later on November 22, 1978. "But It's Still a Newfoundlander!!" screamed the headline. "EPA Changes Hands."

The article explained, much more clearly than the lawyer's letter, that Andrew Crosbie was out as chairman, and Harry Steele of Gander, Newfoundland, was the new president:

> Forty-nine-year-old Harry Raymond Steele, a native of Musgrave Harbour, who worked his way up from highways department labourer to command rank in the Canadian navy, became president and chief executive officer of Eastern Provincial Airways Tuesday.
>
> Mr. Steele also emerged as the largest of the airline's nearly nine hundred shareholders as the result of a $5-million transaction that appeared to put an end to speculation EPA might become the object of a takeover bid by CP Air, which has long sought parallel access with Air Canada into Atlantic Canada.

The article went on, but the reporter, W.C. Callahan, certainly did a masterful job of summing up the entire deal in two concise paragraphs. His observation about CP Air was particularly prescient.

Steele's purchase of EPA was not without its problems, however. "At the time that he bought EPA his main contact within the airline was Harold Wareham. They were kind of like compadres, and Harold was the guy who knew all the inside stuff on the airline and Harry became comfortable with the notion that, if he bought it, they could do something with it. So that was sometime in the late 1970s that he bought it and shortly afterward there was an altercation between Harry and Harold which culminated in a lot of unpleasantness and a court case [which Wareham lost] and all the rest of that," says Doug Rose.

Today, Harold Wareham lives quietly in St. John's. He has no interest in resurrecting old war stories. But in 1996 he had something to say to writer David Napier. While the remarks were descriptive, they showed no sign of bitterness. "Steele's a hard-charger, and some people might feel they're being trampled in the process," says Wareham. "He fights a fair fight, but when he does, he goes for it all. He can leave a lot of people bobbing in his wake, or his slipstream, as it were."

Shortly after taking over EPA, Harry made a couple of take-over moves that were not successful. In 1979 Steele launched an audacious, if ultimately unsuccessful, bid to buy Florida-based National Airlines for $425 million, and the next year hooked up with Algoma Central Railway and a group of Quebec businessmen to try to buy Quebec-based Nordair for $30 million. Finally — and most importantly for employee morale — he took on the giant Canadian Pacific Airlines in a bitter David-and-Goliath battle for control of Atlantic Canada's skies. And won!

Eight

Making a Go of It

He who has the gold makes the rules.
— Harry Steele

From the start, Harry set about making the airline more efficient.

As the journalist Stephen Kimber points out in a 2014 article in *Atlantic Business*: "Steele transformed EPA's $815,000 operating loss the year he bought it into a $4.4-million profit five years later."

Eastern Provincial Airways became the first airline in Canada to ban smoking. Along with doing the crew and passengers a favour in the health department, it also saved money. Cleaning ashtrays in every seat took a lot of time, in particular with an airline that was doing a lot of short hops.

Keeping operations tight meant finding a way to cut EPA's Boeing 737s' fuel burn. Doing so required finding routes that better suited them. The 737 may have been faster, more comfortable, and safer than all the other planes that came before it, but it was ill-suited for many of the routes in Atlantic Canada. They were too short to allow the jet to get up to a high altitude where it could economically cruise. Many of the short hops meant the planes used too much fuel.

"If you're flying the planes half-empty or a third full, you're losing money. On the 737 on a thirty-minute haul, you climb and descend, you hardly have any cruising until you got some long-haul stuff," says Harry.

In the end, the cost of fuel was cut by 10 percent, saving a million and a half dollars a year.

Under The Commander, EPA had the lowest cost structure of any airline in Canada.

That sunny piece of news hid the reality that the fleet was getting older; replacing the aircraft would involve a crippling expense. The person to point that out was Ivan Kilpatrick, the financial guru Harry Steele had brought to EPA. Rather than tackling that problem head on, what Harry Steele did was make the airline a valuable asset, valuable enough for another airline to buy it, before new jet aircraft were needed. That involved a couple of tough battles at Eastern Provincial Airways.

First, the big airlines, Air Canada and CP Air, blocked his plans to expand to Montreal and, more importantly, Toronto. He won that battle. Unions blocked his drive for reasonable hours and lower costs. He won that battle as well.

Airlines were a cozy monopoly in the 1970s and early 1980s. Air Canada was a state-owned airline with a bloated bureaucracy; CP Air, an arm of the giant Canadian Pacific group, the richest conglomerate in the country at the time, was a solid number two. Neither of them wanted competition.

The Halifax to Toronto route was a lucrative run, the eighth busiest in the country, and Air Canada had it all to itself. In the fall of 1979, CP Air applied to the Canadian Transport Commission (CTC) to compete on that route. So did Eastern Provincial Airways.

The national media had never heard of this upstart airline and the man running it. *Maclean's* magazine called him Barry Steele, and the *Financial Post* had his last name as Steel, without the E. The establishment sided with CP Air. It looked like a cake walk. Like many government regulatory bodies, the CTC knew the big players; its members underestimated Harry Steele, as did CP Air.

Their mistake.

Harry Steele went to work. He played the Atlantic Canada card to the hilt and recruited endorsements from all four Conservative premiers from the region. The hearing was held in January of 1980, right in the middle of a rare winter federal election, as Joe Clark's Conservatives were defeated on the issue of Finance Minister John Crosbie's first budget.

At the hearing, there were twice as many people appearing for the EPA side as there were on the CP Air side. It didn't matter, though. In April of 1980, the CTC came down on the side of CP Air. No surprise there. Ottawa bureaucrats supporting the status quo. The essence of the ruling was that the public would be better served by a large airline than a small one: "the present and future public convenience and necessity requires the approval of the CP Air application and the denial of the EPA application."

Harry Steele characterized it as "a kick in the teeth for all Atlantic Canadians." While CP Air's hired hands sat back and congratulated themselves, Harry Steele kept working. It wasn't over until CP Air jets landed in Halifax.

Just after the hearings ended, the federal election brought back Pierre Trudeau and the Liberal Party. "Welcome to the 1980s," said a jubilant Trudeau. Harry Steele welcomed the 1980s by lobbying the cabinet minister from Atlantic Canada in the new government.

David Bruce helped Harry acquire stock in EPA before he took control of the airline. The Toronto stockbroker watched as Harry built that into a success. It took more than just attention to detail at the airline. Harry also had to fight the government to make sure EPA acquired the lucrative routes that, in the end, made Eastern Provincial so attractive to a potential buyer.

"When he had EPA he was really plugged in. He used to be in Ottawa at least once a week. He used to call me from Ottawa," recalls David. "He'd see the prime minister, the minister of transport all the time. He was really plugged in."

At the end of June, the ruling was reversed. Transport Minister Jean-Luc Pepin made the announcement in the House of Commons, giving EPA and Harry Steele a major win.

The decision was cheered on by members of the federal cabinet from the Atlantic provinces: Finance Minister Allan J. MacEachen, a fluent Gaelic-speaking intellectual from Cape Breton, Nova Scotia; Minister of Labour Gerald Regan, an MP from Halifax; and Minister of National Revenue Bill Rompkey of Newfoundland — a politician who was also a lieutenant in the Royal Canadian Navy reserve.

When Bill Rompkey announced the government decision at a press conference in St. John's, Harry Steele was sitting beside him.

The press switched sides and cheered the story of the unlikely victory of the underdog. "As the smoke settles from the political bombshell that blew CP Air out of the skies over Atlantic Canada, the airline may be forgiven for wondering what hit it," wrote Southam News correspondent Brian Butters after the Cabinet decision. "What [CP Air] may eventually come to realize is that it was the unsuspecting victim of a devilishly effective piece of lobbying by some wily politicians from the east coast."

The Halifax journalist and author Stephen Kimber says most of the lobbying was done by none other than Harry Steele.

When the EPA service to Montreal and Toronto started, there was a reception for five hundred people at the Sheraton Centre in Toronto, including 115 people flown in from Atlantic Canada.

Harry's stock market mentor, Seymour Schulich, was on the board of EPA and would soon be chairman of the holding company, Newfoundland Capital Corporation; William Sobey, one of the most prominent businessmen in Atlantic Canada, joined the board; and Harry pinched an Air Canada marketing guru, William Verrier, moving him from London, England, to Gander. Ivan Kilpatrick was the financial and managerial genius Harry brought on board to make sure things ran smoothly. As in the

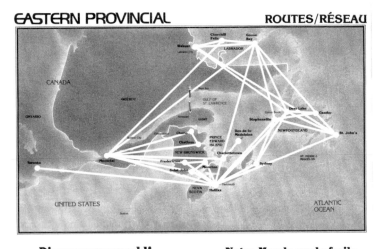

EASTERN PROVINCIAL   ROUTES/RÉSEAU

Discover our world!

For brochures, travel tips,
maps and assistance,
contact:

Tourism New Brunswick
Box 12345, Fredericton, NB E3B 5C3

Newfoundland and Labrador Dept. of Tourism
Box 2016, St. John's, NFLD A1C 5R8

Nova Scotia Dept. of Tourism
Box 456, Halifax, NS B3J 1S9

Ontario Tourism
3rd Floor Hearst, 900, Bay Street, Toronto, Ontario M7A 2E7

Quebec Tourism
2, Place Ville Marie, Suite 6010, Montreal, Quebec
H3B 2C9

PEI Tourism
Box 940, Charlottetown, PEI C1A 7N8

Tourism Office St. Pierre & Miquelon
Box 1207, St. Pierre & Miquelon
Telex 020437

**Eastern Provincial Airways head office
mailing address is:**
Box 5001, Gander, NFLD A1V 1W9
709-256-3941 Telex: 016 43514

Notre Monde rendu facile

Brochures, cartes, horaires, conseils ou assistance,
Eastern Provincial met le tout à votre disposition.
Adressez-vous aux bureaux suivants:

Tourisme Île-du-Prince-Edouard
Case postale 940, Charlottetown, I.-P-E. C1A 7N8

Tourisme Nouveau-Brunswick
Case postale 12345, Fredericton, N.-B. E3B 5C3

Tourisme Nouvelle-Ecosse
Case postale 456, Halifax, N.-E. B3J 1S9

Tourisme Ontario
3e étage Hearst, 900, rue Bay, Toronto, Ontario M7A 2E7

Tourisme Québec
2, Place Ville-Marie, Bureau 6010, Montréal, Québec
H3B 2C9

Office du Tourisme Saint-Pierre et Miquelon
Case postale 1207, Saint Pierre et Miquelon
Telex 020437

Tourisme Terre-Neuve et Labrador
Case postale 2016, St. John, T.-N. A1C 5R8

**L'adresse postale du siège social
d'Eastern Provincial est :**
Case postale 5001, Gander, T.-N. A1V 1W9
709-256-3941 Telex : 016 43514

Route map of Eastern Provincial Airways after its victory to expand to Montreal and Toronto.

navy, Harry believed a commanding officer needed to serve with people he could trust.

Harry Steele was beefing up the board and management team of the once sleepy airline, and at the same time spreading his tentacles into the boardrooms of corporate Canada. It may not have been a plan, but in the rear-view mirror, it sure looks that way.

The stock price of EPA, trading around $1.85 when Harry was accumulating stock before the takeover, was trading at $18 in what investors lovingly call "a ten bagger." That meant Harry

Steele was free of the personal debt he took on to buy EPA and he had a war chest to expand.

The CTC decision resulted in EPA running numerous flights to Montreal and Toronto. With that development, it no longer made sense to maintain the company's base of operations in Gander. There was quite a kerfuffle, however, when the decision was made to run the airline from Halifax rather than Gander.

Discussing the issue, Rob Steele says, "EPA stayed in Gander when the airline had all those milk-run routes. Of course, the airline was very high profile and a big employer in Gander at the time, but once he got those routes to Toronto in the evolution of EPA, it didn't make sense to be in Gander because he'd have to re-position aircraft to Gander and it's costly to do that. It made more sense to have a base more centrally located for his routes in Halifax. So that was quite a controversial thing to take the airline out of Newfoundland to Halifax. It created some real PR issues."

"But we survived," interjects Harry, who is clearly annoyed at the suggestion that he is in any way disloyal to the town where he had a home for fifty years. "It was a tempest in a teapot for six months or a year. Catherine [has] stayed in Gander to this day. Gander is where I do my business and Gander is where I vote."

Many people would have basked in the glory of victory. Harry set about making friends with the enemy. His big rival was Air Canada; it was by far the dominant player. The state-owned airline was also CP Air's worst nightmare. It had bottomless amounts of cash. To fight Air Canada, Harry employed the old military strategy that he had seen used so effectively in the Cold War: *The enemy of my enemy is my friend.*

On September 10, 1982, CP Air and EPA held a joint news conference to announce a deal that had been a year in the making under the code name "East Meets West." The news conference was held via satellite link from Halifax and Vancouver. Though the dual-location news conference gave the impression that it was an announcement of equals, in fact, EPA had the upper hand.

"It was clear to EPA employees and anyone else who analyzed the deal that their little company had emerged as the unquestioned winner in the battle for Atlantic Canadian skies, and that CP Air was simply being allowed to skulk quietly out of the east with its corporate tail between its legs," wrote the author and journalist Stephen Kimber in an analysis of the company.

There was a bonus to the agreement: in its routes to Montreal and Toronto, EPA could do a "codeshare" with CP Air, which meant passengers could fly seamlessly into the CP Air system.

"Mr. Steele said he expects the integration [with CP Air] to produce a significant increase in profit and load factor," said an article in the *Globe and Mail*. "The merger should mean a big increase in EPA's presence in the Montreal and Toronto market and a renewal of its request for access to Ottawa."

The *Globe* said the only benefit for the loser, CP Air, would be that EPA would funnel passengers into its routes from Montreal and Toronto.

The future was looking bright for EPA, but, in fact, there were dark storm clouds on the horizon. Ever since Steele had bought the company, it had, in effect, been operating at two levels. On the public level, Eastern Provincial was the epitome of the upbeat but unlikely corporate success story so loved by journalists. Eastern Provincial itself helped foster that image, which, after all, was not only truthful as far as it went but was also good for investor confidence.

That perception of the company was reinforced in the 1981 NCC annual report, which read like a glowing statistical sampler: "In every month, [reduced fuel use] producing an [annual] $835,000 saving to the company, while flight crew utilization improved by 9 percent in the cockpit and 6 percent in the cabin," the report notes with pride, "we improved our boardings over last year, with an overall margin gain of 4.6 percent on boardings. We added sixty-seven million seat miles (10 percent) to our capacity and slightly increased the load factor to 56.9 percent. Boeing 737 daily utilization increased from its already high 1980 level of 9.05 hours per day to 9.29 hours per day in 1981. For the Hawker Siddeley 748, utilization improved dramatically from 3.56 hours per day to 5.16 hours per day." And on and on.

The rate of fuel burn had been reduced. Most important, of course, was the fact that the airline's net income had increased nearly four times over its 1980 level of $1,242,000 to $4,402,000 in 1981.

At the private level, within the upper reaches of corporate management, there was a frightening recognition that the journalists' and analysts' rosy forecasts of future prosperity were based on a kind of smoke-and-mirrors illusion that there would simply be a continuation of the present. In fact, Eastern Provincial was already operating on borrowed time.

Shortly after he arrived at the company in 1979, Ivan Kilpatrick had discovered what he called "an absolute bomb that was about to go off, two bombs, in fact, one was a nuclear bomb, probably hydrogen, and the other was just an ordinary nuclear bomb."

The ordinary nuclear bomb threat involved the company's fleet. EPA's jets, which had been obtained back in 1970, would soon have to be replaced. EPA had originally purchased one of these planes outright; it leased five others. When they were put in service, they were worth five million dollars each, with interest calculated at 7 percent over a fifteen-year amortization period. Based on an estimation that the planes were flying an average of three thousand hours per year, the company determined that the planes were costing the airline $182.99 per hour to operate. That figure was used by EPA as a guide in setting the fares it charged passengers.

The cost to replace those airplanes, however, was three times as much as it had been in 1970, and interest on the new fifteen-million-dollar price tag would have to be calculated at more than twice the 1970 interest rate, or 15 percent, and the loans themselves would probably have to be paid off in ten years instead of fifteen.

The long and short of all the fancy number-crunching was that a plane costing $182.99 an hour to run today would soon have to be replaced by an aircraft that would cost $996.26 an hour — nearly five and a half times as much. The airline, therefore, would either have to tightly squeeze its other costs to hold down fares or push fares through the roof.

There was another solution, it seemed: EPA could sell the one plane it had purchased outright and purchase two of its five leased jets for their depreciated value of one million dollars each, thereby reducing the real replacement cost of those planes. However, that seemingly attractive option was, in fact, not an option. The reality was — this was Kilpatrick's hydrogen bomb — the three remaining leased planes contained an option clause that virtually forced EPA to buy them back at the end of the lease period for "fair market value." What that meant was that when the leases ran out on December 31, 1984, EPA would have to buy its own used airplanes again for more than they had originally paid for them. By the time it finished "buying" each airplane twice, it would have spent millions and it would have wound up with a twenty-five-year-old jet.

Despite those twin time bombs, Kilpatrick and Steele were undaunted. *All we have to do is get the guys onside,* Kilpatrick convinced himself at the time. *They'll see the problems. There's lots of scope here for winning. Business looks good; we'll simply re-finance the airline and keep going.*

He had one other problem to solve first: work rules and pay for the pilots of EPA.

Nine

The Pilots' Strike

Overdressed, oversexed, overpaid bus drivers.
— A quote about EPA pilots often
attributed to Harry Steele but in fact
spoken by an EPA board member

There was no greater test of the mettle of Harry Steele than the pilot's strike at Eastern Provincial Airways. It was a battle fought first at the negotiating table, then in the media, and finally on the front lines of EPA's operations. The pilots were members of CALPA, the Canadians Airline Pilots Association. It was a strong union and had won many battles over the years, in particular with Air Canada, which had caved in to demands and short strikes over the years.

Takey is a Harry Steele word. It is not in the *Oxford English Dictionary*, but Harry offers a clear definition for it: a takey is someone who wants more than their share and digs in to get it. He saw the pilots' union as a bunch of takeys.

Harry wanted the pilots to fly more hours; the union said that its members would only agree to do so if the company agreed to a set of demands put forward by them. Harry Steele decided he would not give in. When it was reported that he called the pilots "glorified bus drivers" — though he denied he was the one who said it — the union stepped up its war of words. They underestimated their adversary. The man from Musgrave Harbour was not for turning.

Every reporter who covered the EPA strike latched on to the bus driver story. It immediately portrayed Harry Steele as the callous boss ridiculing his striking employees. But it might have struck a chord with the public who knew airline pilots were making more than double the average wage and then some.

The reality is Harry never said it. In an article written by David Napier in 1996, Harry went out of his way to deny the legend. Napier describes the meeting at Harry's office: "It's not that I am trying to run away from those words, it's just that I didn't say them," says Steele, as he bellows to his assistant, "Veronica! Get me the overdressed, oversexed bus driver file."

Moments later, Steele is pulling newspaper clippings from a manila folder that prove he never dubbed striking airline pilots at his old company, Eastern Provincial Airways, a bunch of "overdressed, oversexed, overpaid bus drivers." It sounds like something the outspoken Steele, who has had more than his share of union dust-ups, would say but the words weren't his; EPA board member Jean Claude Hebert uttered the infamous phrase that brought negotiations with the pilots' union to a fever pitch back in 1983. The comment, however, has now become entrenched in Steele legend.

Here is a public notice put out by the company, under the photograph and signature of H.R. Steele, president and chief executive officer. It explains the situation in clear, direct language:

The Eastern Provincial Pilots' Strike

On January 27th, 1983 when the Management of Eastern Provincial put a two-year offer to its jet pilots of an increase of 14.6 percent along with a request which would have increased hard flying hours from an average of 51 per month to 55 per month, the Company's CALPA pilots stopped work and went on strike.

The increase in hard flying hours requested by the company is far below the Department of Transport limits of 120 hours.

It was intended by CALPA that the strike action of January 27th would shut down the Airline and cut off services to places like Labrador, [the] Magdalen Islands, and St. Pierre and Miquelon, whose residents depend entirely upon the airline for transportation.

They thought the shutdown would raise such a public outcry and put such financial pressure on the Airline that, at any cost to the public and the Company, we would be forced to accede to their demands.

Instead of accepting this shutdown, we informed CALPA that:

Long range survival of the Airline required improved pilot productivity, during the strike we would operate the airline, and if the strike were protracted, we would hire new pilots.

One month after the strike had begun, with 40 percent of the schedule in operation, the Company began the process of carefully selecting and hiring new pilots. As of today, May 2nd, this process continues. Scheduled operations have reached 70 percent of normal and new pilots are on the payroll. We expect to fly 100 percent of the schedule by summer.

CALPA now wants us to get rid of the new pilots. Our position is, they came to us in good faith to carry out our obligation to satisfy public convenience and necessity as required by our licences. They have lived up to their end of the bargain, and we will live up to ours.

A Philosophy of Work

Newfoundland Capital Corporation continues to stand behind the following philosophy of work for the employees of all its Divisions.

Our obligation to protect jobs for all employees imposes a requirement not to accede to inordinate demands of some employees.

The airline industry is in serious trouble and will continue in serious trouble until airline fares and airline costs fall to the level which the public is willing to pay.

Costs can be lowered either by layoffs or by increased productivity. The Company will stress productivity because it has the minimum cost and the maximum benefit for everybody, the public, the shareholders, all employees, including our pilots.

That was one side of the story. The pilots looked at things another way. You could argue that the pilots were winning the media war, in the local press and on national television. Here are two examples, the first from Jo Ann Napier's article "Strikers Have 'Drawn the Line,'" published in the February 3, 1983, edition of the *Halifax Chronicle Herald*:

"Safety aboard Eastern Provincial Airways (EPA) flights could be compromised by union acceptance of management proposals," the spokesman for striking EPA pilots said Wednesday.

During a press conference in Halifax, Captain Keith Lacey said the 92 pilots who went on strike Jan. 26 have "drawn the line" with contract concessions over working hours, daily duty times, and rest periods.

The news conference followed announcements that EPA has contracted out pilots and equipment from Austin Airways of Timmins, Ont., to handle "essential" flight services.

"You don't hold the pilot profession up for ransom just because times are hard," said Capt. Lacey, adding that striking members of the Canadian Air Lines Pilot Association (CALPA) will not waver in their bargaining stance.

"It is the passengers who have been held hostage by CALPA," countered EPA spokesman Merv Russell, during a telephone interview from Gander, Nfld.

He suggested EPA clientele who rely on the "essential" services provided by the regional [airline] were placed in a difficult position by the pilots' strike.

Mr. Russell noted that management opted for a "moderate stance" in the dispute by contracting out, rather than hiring, the Austin Airways pilots.

He disagreed with suggestions that safety standards may be threatened by the company's proposal to increase EPA pilots credited flying time from 80 to 85 hours per month.

"Eighty-five hours per month is certainly safe," said Mr. Russell, adding that pilots at Nordair carry that workload, which is within Ministry of Transport guidelines.

But the union spokesman said the company proposal is "just a case of asking for too much, too soon."

"There are some limits, and we've reached most of those limits," said Capt. Lacey.

Regarding EPA's move to bring in outside pilots, Capt. Lacey said it is "unfortunate" the company deemed it necessary to bring in outside people rather [than] try to settle the dispute.

EPA has contracted Austin Airways to pilot three flight routes and to provide its own Hawker Siddeley

748 turboprop airplanes for one of those flights —
from Montreal to the northern New Brunswick
towns of Chatham and Charlo.

On March 31, 1983, Harry Steele and Keith Lacey went toe
to toe on *The Journal*, a nightly television program that aired after
The National. (The author worked on *The Journal* at the time.)
What follows is an exact transcript of that interview. HS is Harry
Steele; KL is Keith Lacey; PK is Peter Kent; and MF, Mary Lou
Finlay, the main interviewer.

MF: Five weeks ago pilots at Eastern Provincial Airways
went on strike cutting Atlantic services in half. The
labour dispute has degenerated into charges, counter-
charges, name-calling and rebuttals in newspaper
advertisements. What's surprising about the bitterness of this strike is that the two sides never seem
to be too far apart.

PK: With no settlement in sight, Eastern Provincial
Airways took matters into its own hands this week
hiring pilots to replace those on strike.

[Video showing strikers hitting Tilden rental van with
hammers and axes: "C'mon, you bunch of scabs."]

PK: The first eight pilots arrived for work in Halifax
where they were met by picketing EPA employees.
EPA's high-flying, free-enterprise boss, Harry
Steele, says the pilots hired through the strike will
stay with EPA and that those still on strike will have
to take their chances of finding jobs when the strike
is over. The central issue in the strike is productivity. The company wants to increase the number of
hours the pilots fly from eighty to eighty-five hours
a month and to reduce time between flights.

In the fight for public sympathy, both sides took their case to the public with newspaper ads. The company took out this one, which says pilots are only working fifteen days a month and the company is asking for just one more day's work.

The man behind Eastern Provincial Airways is Harry Steele. He took over the perennial money loser five years ago and turned the carrier around to record a profit last year. The pilots argue that the profit column shows the airline is already more productive than most and while the pilots have shown a willingness to be flexible, Harry Steele hasn't given an inch.

MF: In an attempt to end the strike the pilots have said that they are willing to go back to work under the old contract. That offer was rejected by the company. We have linked the two sides in this dispute: Harry Steele is president of EPA and Captain Keith Lacey is a captain who has flown for fourteen years and is head of its Pilots Association.

Mr. Steele, the pilots have said they are willing to go back to work for you, with no increases. Why won't you take them back?

HS: The issue, Mary Lou, is one of productivity. We must have eighty-five hours a month, and if the pilots want to give us eighty-five hours a month, we'll take them back.

MF: Captain Lacey, why did you reject that demand from your company?

KL: We didn't reject that demand from the company. At no time did we reject that demand and I'd say to Mr. Steele right now that if all he wants is eighty-five hours a month over our old contract, I will give it to him right here and now on television. He can have his eighty-five hours over the old contract with no other changes. I will stand by my word and give him his eighty-five hours with no other changes in our old contract. I say that now, and I mean it.

MF: Mr. Steele?

HS: Yes, well the contract is very thick and there's more than one issue. We need the eighty-five hours, and I can't say to Captain Lacey we're going to take out everything else, but that's the crux of the matter.

MF: Captain Lacey has said you can have it, so what's keeping you apart?

HS: Yes, but Captain Lacey has said that a few times before but I've not seen him offer it. What he's offering in the latest proposal is something less than eighty-five hours.

KL: I'd like to cut in right there … that's not right, Mr. Steele, and you know it. I've offered you eighty-five hours several times in different forms. You say you want eighty-five hours. That's not an increase of five hours, it's an increase of ten hours in some months, and we've offered you just now in the latest offer eighty-five hours per month; we offered it to you in a newspaper ad, and we're offering it to you again. If the old contract wasn't good enough for you and all you want is eighty-five hours flying per month on the jet with the salary you give us and that's your figure, … then I ask you 'you have it.' Why are we not back to work?

HS: The fact of the matter is that as I understand it, Captain Lacey, you have not offered the eighty-five hours and if you've got that to offer you had better go back to your committee and negotiate with them,

I'm sure they will give it to you. That is the fundamental issue is eighty-five hours. There may be other considerations.

KL: The fact is that the company is leading everybody to believe … it's not the major issue. The company is leading everyone, the public included, and the pilots that the only problem here is five more hours of work. You put a very expensive ad in the newspaper, and we answered it: *We accept, the issue is now settled.* But it's not settled.

MF: Captain Lacey, what do you think are the other demands that the company won't talk about?

KL: The company has made a long list of demands. They gave them to us on the fifteenth of October, and we still have them. They have totally ignored any proposals we have put on the table. They have them, and they still have them.

MF: What are the other demands and what are the things you object to?

KL: We object to the company wanting to increase their supervisory pilots to a number that they so designate. They want to increase our landings, and they want to increase our duty period and decrease our rest periods. The whole issue that they want … And they chalk it all up to five more hours of work.

MF: Mr. Steele, it seems as though there is more to this than just the eighty-five hours a month.

HS: Sure there are other things when people work, there's more to it than salary and hours, and that is the contentious issue is one of productivity. The fact of the matter is that people should be working more than two weeks a month. I think that eighty-five hours …

and that's not "hard time," that's "credited time," so it only works out to about fifty hours a month actually flying.

MF: I'm really confused here now because you say that is the main issue, the crux of the whole thing, and we hear Captain Lacey saying "You can have that." Yet nothing is happening.

HS: Well, Captain Lacey has offered that before and I —

KL: It was offered before, and it was offered in good faith, and it still is.

HS: You've only offered it, Captain Lacey, on radio and television, and your latest proposal as I understand it now … did you offer eighty-five hours in your proposal today?

KL: I most certainly did so.

HS: You did? Well, that's not my understanding.

KL: The whole thing has gotten a little bit "low" here with different press releases and company releases and pilots being referred to as everything from bus drivers to technicians. We have offered this company — Mr. Steele says that his only problem is productivity and the shareholders and we have our careers here, our lives. We have devoted as much to this airline and have as much invested in it as Mr. Steele does.

MF: If I'm not misreading you, Mr. Lacey, I think you're saying now, and you've said before, that you didn't think the company really wanted to negotiate. Let me put that to Mr. Steele: Do you want to settle this?

HS: Yes, we do want to settle. We want Captain Lacey and all of his pilots back, and we want them back very badly.

MF: Mr. Steele, if that eighty-five hours a month is on the table, is this over?

HS: Well, if it's on the table, as far as I'm concerned it's over because if these other things that he addressed are looked after as well. But the major stumbling block, as I understand it, is the eighty-five hours, and unless we get eighty-five hours for $83,741 a year for the captains, there will be no settlement.

MF: Captain Lacey, is that eighty-five hours a month on the table?

KL: It was interesting just then to hear Mr. Steele say, "If the eighty-five hours is the major stumbling block." And then he said, "In addition to all the other things." Mr. Steele knows the eighty-five hours is the major stumbling block because I've just given him all the other things. He knew that this afternoon.

MF: Okay, is the eighty-five on the table?

KL: It's on the table, but it's not on the table with all the other things, no.

HS: Well, is it there or isn't it? Is the eighty-five hours on the table?

KL: If that's the only thing you want....

HS: Is it there?

KL: It's not there with all the other things you want, no.

HS: Okay, well then I suggest to you that it's not there.

KL: It most certainly is so there.

MF: Gentlemen, I thank you both for this. It sounds as though you're not that far apart. I may be inexperienced, but I look forward to this in the next day or two.

HS: Yes, I do too.

The consensus is that Harry Steele lost that battle. Keith Lacey was more at home on television, and it showed, maybe not in the transcript of the interview, but certainly on the screen. That was a battle in a long war that, in the end, the company won, and the union lost.

Rex Murphy, no stranger to television, worked as a reporter in Newfoundland at the time of the strike. He says Harry Steele is "tough as a nail." "Harry went through the picket line every single day. The idea that you could physically or morally blackmail him was never going to be," says Rex. He says Harry had too much to lose to give in. "Everything was hanging by a thread; he had a family, and he had borrowed to get The Albatross and then he ends up with this EPA airline from the Crosbie bankruptcies. Nothing was easy."

More than a dozen years later, Keith Lacey was interviewed by David Napier about life with Harry. Though the two men were fierce opponents at the time, Lacey was surprisingly laid back:

> "I like Steele and enjoyed being around him," says Captain Keith Lacey, who represented the Canadian Air Line Pilots' Association (CALPA) during the 1983 strike at EPA. However, Lacey adds that Steele's "militaristic style" often meant that senior recruits to the East Coast airline "weren't sure if they were joining the Forces or EPA management." And below the executive level, unionized employees were worried not only about future changes in an industry that was due to deregulate but about what they perceived as their boss's anti-union attitude.

Well, maybe Lacey harboured a touch of bitterness.

John French was a pilot with EPA who defied the union and kept flying throughout the strike. He started flying for EPA in Greenland in the early 1960s and then went to work with them on the mainland in 1966. French's long history with the airline was part of the reason he defied the union and worked during the strike.

French first met Harry a short time after the Steeles bought The Albatross Hotel. "We used to spend a lot of time there when we were on layovers, and I would see him there having breakfast. EPA was very small, and we would see him, or the previous president, Keith Miller, and we were almost on a first-name basis being such a small company."

John French was involved with the union at Eastern Provincial and, at one point, was the union local president. But his relationship with the union changed when the strike began. "It was a very difficult time. I wasn't involved in an executive capacity, but when the strike occurred I think the union went out for about a month, which I supported without any question whatsoever. As they stayed out, it became obvious that Harry couldn't keep the airline going under that situation, so he told the union that he was going to bring in outside workers to fly the airplanes. There was no doubt in my mind that he was serious and that, if he did it, things were only going to get worse.

"I advised the union leadership that, after a month, it was time to bring the membership back to work before that happened and live to fight another day but, of course, my advice was not taken. The union leadership had very different views of it. So I told them that I disagreed with their position on that issue and that if they continued to insist on keeping the membership out that would be a decision that I could not support and I would have no choice but to resign my membership in the union and go back to work, which is what I did. I want to make it perfectly clear that the decision was made by my wife and me and not with Harry or any of the EPA management whatsoever.

"That strike turned into one of the bitterest strikes in the history of Canadian labour. Friendships were lost; I had best friends there who never spoke to me again. It was very bitter, and there's nothing good that can be said about it. I want to make it perfectly clear that both sides were to blame for it: Harry and the EPA management were wrong to bring in outside workers, and I think that he grossly underestimated the [resolve of the] union, and I think the union was just as wrong in underestimating him and his management team. It was just a situation where both were at loggerheads, and I guess no compromise was going to be made and it was all very sad.

"There were a number of court cases, and the courts ruled that Harry was justified in bringing the outside workers in, and another court overturned that. It was the end of EPA, and there were certainly no winners, with the possible exception of Harry, who was a winner financially because he ended up selling the airline for a sizeable profit. But there were no real winners; families were torn apart, and it was just a bad scene."

John French stayed in touch with Harry Steele, who always remembered him. "Harry told me after the strike that if there was anything he could ever do for me not to hesitate to ask him. I took him up on that offer, and he kept his word. He was very kind and generous to my late wife, Estelle, and me, and in that regard, I have nothing but good to say about him. I have a winter home in San Juan, Puerto Rico, and have made some very good friends there and once I invited a couple of my friends up to Canada for the first time and I asked Harry if there was any chance of taking them to his fishing camp and there were no questions asked."

Eventually, CP Air bought Eastern Provincial. That deal was a building block for expansion and growth. The family reaction was surprising.

"I think there was a great relief in the family. Obviously financially it worked out very well but, for me being very young at that point, it was one of the happiest days of my life because at that time we had gone through a long period of financial uncertainty plus incredibly bitter labour strikes and living in a small town it was tough," says John Steele.

You might think people at school would have picked on him during the strike, but that was not the case. "Everybody at high school always treated me very well. Later at (Memorial) university you'd have somebody who the odd time might say something to you, but within the town of Gander itself, I have to say that it was not a problem. You had people whose parents were out on strike, but they always treated me very well. I never had anybody give me a hard time in Gander about it."

The family may not have suffered attacks from their neighbours and peers, but Harry certainly did. There were even troubles with the Newfoundland government, Brian Peckford in particular. Peckford was premier of Newfoundland from 1979 to 1989, which, apart from a brief period in 1978, covers the time Harry Steele ran Eastern Provincial Airways and was on the board of CP Air.

Rex Murphy puts it down to a clash of personalities.

"Steele was one of these really independent personalities and some of these strong-arm premiers, and Peckford was in his day, don't like secondary characters. Steele wasn't established yet, and this was when everything was fragile. Air Canada was gunning for him too."

Harry ran a tight ship at EPA, but he knew the airline would never be a big money spinner. "You don't make money running an airline; you make money when you sell it."

Harry started his venture with EPA in 1978 as a man with a hotel, a middling-sized stock portfolio, and a mortgage on the family home. He ended with a profit of $20 million in 1982 after just four years. That $20 million went to Newfoundland Capital Corporation, not to Harry personally. It was the seed capital that started Harry Steele and his company on a buying spree over the next decade into even more profitable businesses, first in transportation, then newspapers and radio.

Harry Steele would never look back.

Ten

Travel with CP Air

Travel with CP Air is a global affair.
— Company ad slogan

There is a coarse expression about having your enemy inside the tent rather than outside it. CP Air welcomed The Commander to its board in 1984, soon after it bought Eastern Provincial.

The company, founded in 1942 as Canadian Pacific Airlines, had changed its name to CP Air in 1968. In 1986 CP Air changed its name back to Canadian Pacific Airlines. The next year it merged with Pacific Western Airlines and Nordair to become Canadian Airlines International — a bit of a mouthful for the marketing department to deal with — to reflect what the airline saw as its strength: its international routes. It covered places that its rival, Air Canada, did not, such as South America, Japan, and Australia, as well as other locations.

Despite the mergers and acquisitions and attempts to position the airline as a real competitor to Air Canada, the company was having real problems. It hoped that Harry could help sort them out.

Harry soldiered on with the others on the board, and after a dozen years, he was named the non-executive chairman of Canadian Airlines International, replacing Rhys Eyton. People in non-executive positions are not usually supposed to meddle in the nitty-gritty of the running of the airline. However, Harry was never one to worry about getting his hands dirty. "If he's a figurehead, it'll be the first time in his life he's been one," says Lyndon Watkins, founder of *Frank Magazine*, in an article by David Napier in 1996.

His close friend Craig Dobbin, a fellow Newfoundlander, saw Harry's appointment as a win for the home team. "For someone from Newfoundland to be appointed the chairman of what is basically a western Canadian airline is a tribute. He's now a player on the international scene," said Dobbin at the time.

It may have been a personal coup for Harry, but there was not much to celebrate at the company. There was no doubt Canadian Airlines International was in deep trouble at the time. The year before Harry took on the chairman's role the airline lost $194.7 million. In today's dollars, that's $302 million, according to the Bank of Canada's inflation calculator.

Harry thought he knew the problem. "We don't have a revenue problem, we have a cost problem," Harry told David Napier. "We've got to increase productivity and get our costs in line, that's the game."

Because of the strikes at Eastern Provincial, there was an assumption that Harry Steele was anti-union and would move to get tough with pilots, flight attendants, and machinists. He told David Napier as he entered the job that he didn't see unions as a problem. "All the companies I am involved in are highly union-ized: steelworkers, paperworkers, longshoremen, communications workers. I have no problems working with unions."

Labour was not the only cost that was a problem, however. Many things plagued the airline, including the devastation of the made-in-Canada recession of the early 1990s, brought on in part by rising interest rates as the Bank of Canada tried to control real estate inflation. The central bank's gambit worked, but many companies suffered, including Newfoundland Capital Corporation, which had a debt crisis of its own in 1993.

The situation at Canadian would prove to be even more diffi-cult than it was for NCC, but Harry knew that going in. "It's a tough, tough business, but, frankly, I enjoy it," he said. "There are so many moving parts, so many things go right, and an awful lot of things go wrong." Harry said then, and he repeated it in 2017, that running an airline is no way to make money. He made money when he sold his airline, as did other entrepreneurs such as Max Ward of Wardair.

"It's like Don Carty once put it: 'This isn't a business, it's a disease,'" quipped Harry.

When a reporter suggested that things were so bad that Canadian Airlines International could go under, Harry blasted back with a stern defence. "Not that many years ago we had seven carriers and some of them made money. All this talk about there not being room for two carriers is balderdash. The only one who advocates for that is [former Air Canada chairman] Hollis Harris."

Harry was not the only smart businessman on the board. There was Donald Carty, scion of a Canadian hotel family, who successfully ran American Airlines; Peter Lougheed, the ex-premier of Alberta; and John Cassady, then head of CTV who went on to rebuild Corus. But all the king's horses and all the king's men couldn't put things together again. Canadian Airlines International gave in, pushed to the financial limit, and it threw in the towel when in 2000 it was acquired by Air Canada. With the demise of Canadian, Harry left the airline business behind for the first time in twenty-two years.

Eleven

Clarke Transport

His best deal was probably Clarke Trans
port. Because he bought it right.
— Rob Steele, who as an eighteen-
year-old watched his father make the
Clarke Transport deal

In 1981, while Harry still owned and operated EPA, he bought
Clarke Transport. The company was part of the holdings of Clarke
Steamships of Montreal, which operated a variety of transportation businesses, involving ships, trucks, and rail. With the purchase of Clarke, NCC became involved in all forms of ground
transportation, as well as shipping.

The deal was emblematic of the way Harry operated: find value,
something that is either underpriced or under pressure, and move
to buy it. Running the operation would be someone else's job,
a person he trusted; Harry kept an eye on things, but his main
focus was on finding opportunity and taking advantage of it. The
Commander of Newfoundland Capital Corporation.

Kevin Griffin, in a yet-to-be-published work, "St. Lawrence
Saga: The Clarke Steamship Story," describes the takeover as a
shocker in the tightknit shipping community:

In a surprise announcement on October 10, 1981, it
was revealed that Newfoundland Capital Corporation

(NCC) of Gander, owner of Eastern Provincial Airways, was to acquire all the shares of Northmount Holdings, as Clarke Traffic Services was now known. This, in turn, included 100 percent control of the Clarke group of companies, its half-interest in Newfoundland Steamships and its third-interest and management contract for the Halterm container terminal in Halifax.

The Clark Transport deal was finalized in the restaurant of the old Hotel Newfoundland. Harry often brought one of his boys along, and on this day it was eighteen-year-old Rob Steele, who at the time was studying at Memorial University. No one at the table knew that the teenager sitting there would have a hand in disposing of the company almost two decades later.

Rob has a sharp picture of what went on that day. "I remember going to the restaurant and chatting with Mr. Clarke, and Seymour Schulich was there too. I remember my father doing the deal, and I think it was twelve million dollars. But in retrospect now, remembering how deals work, there was a little reception upstairs so the deal must have been consummated before that meeting at the Hotel Newfoundland. My recollection is that it was quite emotional for Mr. Clarke."

Rob could see that Stanley Clarke was upset about parting with a slice of the business that his grandfather had started at the turn of the twentieth century. The Clarkes were a family of energetic entrepreneurs; they had built pulp mills and hydroelectric plants near Sept Îles on Quebec's North Shore. They started their shipping line in 1921 and expanded into all forms of transportation along the St. Lawrence and beyond.

The Clarke family was also involved in the development of the Anglo-Newfoundland Development Company, the forestry company set up to supply paper for London's *Daily Mail*. Sitting at that table at the Hotel Newfoundland were the son and grandson of Stanley and Katie Steele, who worked in the woods for Anglo-Newfoundland. That history wasn't on the table, though; the assets of the Clarke empire were.

Newfoundland Capital bought the non-shipping assets of the Montreal-based firm. That included a 50 percent interest in Halterm, an acronym for Halifax Terminals, a container operation in the Port of Halifax. There was also a trucking company, a ferry service on the St. Lawrence River, and Oceanex, a shipping company serving ports from Montreal to St. John's and Halifax.

Atlantic Business wrote its take on the anatomy of the deal.

> After looking at various takeover possibilities across Canada and the United States, a search firm in Montreal last summer suggested Northmount Holdings, the investment holding company of brothers Stanley and Brock Clarke, which controlled Clarke Transport Canada of Montreal.
>
> Clarke has been an enormously successful company, with transportation interests ranging from management of the Halterm container terminal to ferries and coastal shipping involvements, trucking, railcar, and even automobile dealerships.
>
> It was a perfect match. Clarke was keen to sell; Steele equally keen to buy. It will cost the company $18.5 million and give it assets worth $27 million. Final details were worked out between Steele and Stanley Clarke over lunch at the Mount Royal Club in Montreal. It was their only meeting. Clarke then flew off to an appointment in China, but he was promised to remain as chairman of NCC's Clarke Transport subsidiary for at least a year.
>
> At sixty-four, Stanley was now reaching retirement age and had decided to sell. His two sons, Desmond

and Donald, were working in the industry and his daughter, Rosemary, was at school. Desmond, the elder brother, was now in Bermuda, while Donald had joined Clarke and was vice president of the pool-car division at the time of the sale.

A mini-Canadian Pacific?

That was how the Halifax-based magazine *Atlantic Business* described Newfoundland Capital Corporation in its issue of January–February 1982. An exaggerated piece of hometown boosterism, but their description of NCC's operation was quite concise and accurate:

> NCC has been in existence for barely a year, and even in the Atlantic Region, it isn't exactly a household name. But it owns such well-known companies as Eastern Provincial Airways and Clarke Transport Canada Inc., as well as such lesser lights as Maritime Petroleum Ltd. and Atlantic Inns. In addition, Steele has other personal business interests ranging from real estate to helicopters.
>
> With its regional airline, a 50 percent interest in a coastal shipping company, one-third ownership of Halterm, operators of the Halifax container terminal, 775 highway trucks, tractors, and trailers, a successful railway pool car division, and a score of road, rail and shipping terminals spread across Eastern Canada and beyond, NCC is one of the most varied and integrated transportation companies in Canada. It is a mini-Canadian Pacific. And the ambitions of its guiding light are no less than theirs.
>
> The group employs nearly two thousand people. Its sales this year will be over $150 million and its pre-tax profits, based on a 1981 performance of

between $3.5 million and $4 million, should be at least $6 million.

Steele personally owns 47 percent of NCC. Two other directors, chairman Seymour Schulich and Calgary oilman John Fleming, each own 7 percent and a group of life insurance companies, pension plans, and other central Canadian–based financial institutions 10 percent.

One of the people who convinced Harry to buy Clarke Transport was Ivan Kilpatrick, an academic who Harry brought on to help him run Eastern Provincial Airways. Doug Rose, who worked with Harry for many years as director of mergers and acquisitions and who also wrote the boss's speeches and the annual reports of Newfoundland Capital Corporation, says Ivan Kilpatrick provided Harry with some of the theoretical know-how he didn't have. "Harry once told me 'Rose, I knew I needed help on the finance side and the management of the businesses.'

"Ivan was then retired and teaching business and finance at the University of Prince Edward Island. Harry went over and tried to recruit him, and Ivan turned him down the first time. He thought about it some more, and finally they got moving together. Ivan joined Harry while Harry still had EPA and he became vice-president of finance. It was Ivan Kilpatrick who was the lead hand in the acquisition of Clarke from Stanley Clarke. Harry often attributes the success of his operation to Ivan. Harry once said to me, 'Rose, I needed a guy who could keep me from trying to get my arms around too many things at once.'

"Because he was so full of energy and wanted to do everything, he knew he needed a tough right-hand man who could give him good advice and tell him when he was trying to do too much and keep him in line."

In many ways, Kilpatrick was around to tell Harry Steele sometimes what he didn't want to hear: that some deals were not worth chasing. Some of Kilpatrick's critics say he was in love with old-style industrial businesses; he couldn't get his head around ephemeral things, especially radio.

But Ivan was loyal to Harry, and that worked both ways.

"Harry credits Ivan for a lot of the good that came out of NCC, and if you had met him in earlier days, he would often reminisce about Ivan and what he had done to help build the company," said Rose.

Clarke Transport was a business with a solid industrial base: things you could see and touch. It was built to feed cargo to Clarke Steamships, but by the time Harry purchased it, it was a transport business with many separate pieces.

Atlantic Container Express, also known by its initials, ACE, was part of the complex transit mix; even the ownership was complex. Stanley Clarke kept a 25 percent ownership in the business, meaning ACE Lines was a partnership that came with the Clarke business, of which NCC owned 25 percent. Atlantic

Clarke Transport: the second big business.

Container operated a couple of container vessels and shipped containers from Montreal and Halifax to Newfoundland and back again.

"ACE was still called that when I arrived there; there was a Newfoundland partner, Fednav was a partner, so was Clarke, and these were the four partners in the business. It was run by a very successful CEO whose name was Gilles Champagne, who was quite an operator," says Doug Rose. Eventually ACE morphed into what is now Oceanex, and that meant Fednav, the large Montreal deep-sea operator, was also involved as a partner.

In August 1982, *Seaports & the Shipping World* gave a Newfoundland perspective in its "Signals from St. John's" column:

> A new container company, Atlantic Container Express, was recently announced by Harry Steele, president of Newfoundland Capital Corporation, and Peter Outerbridge, president of A. Harvey & Co.
>
> Atlantic Container Express was formed to compete with the highly subsidized Terra Transport, a subsidiary of Canadian National. It combines the resources of Atlantic Freight Lines and Newfoundland Steamships and will operate three ice-classed container ships between Newfoundland and Montreal.
>
> The *Catalina* and the *Lady M.A. Crosbie* will operate on a four-day frequency between Montreal and St. John's, and the *Bonaventure II* will operate once weekly between Corner Brook and Montreal.
>
> Gilles Champagne, who has been in the freight business for twenty years or more and has been with Atlantic Freight Lines since its inception in 1980, was named president.
>
> The new company expects to handle around 400,000 tons of cargo during its first year of operation [through] a centralized facility in St. John's Harbour.

At the same time that these new ships began operation, the *Chimo* performed the last voyage of any mainline Clarke ship when it left Montreal on August 9, 1982, for Rae Point, Melville Island, under charter to C.A. Crosbie Shipping. After returning to Montreal at the conclusion of this voyage, the *Chimo* cleared for lay-up at Sorel, and four days later the *Cabot* (another Clarke ship and no relation to HMCS *Cabot*) was towed from its temporary berth in Montreal to lay up alongside the *Chimo*. The only majority-owned Clarke shipping concern was now La Traverse Rivière-du-Loup–St-Siméon Ltée and its Trans-St-Laurent (the ferry service across the St. Lawrence River).

At the point where the ferry operation operated, the St. Lawrence River is twenty-seven kilometres wide, with spectacular scenery. It offers a perfect opportunity for whale watching. For tourists, the trip across the St. Lawrence is wonderful; for those trying to make a profit ferrying tourists and others across the river, however, the passage is rather disappointing.

Despite the poor results from the ferry operation, Clarke Transport was a hugely successful investment for Harry and Newfoundland Capital. The operating units, with some exceptions, made significant contributions to the holding company's profits every year. And when the parts were sold off almost two decades later, the original investment seemed even more astute.

Some parts of the business took more tending than others. As with all his investments, except for Eastern Provincial Airways, Harry was involved in the deal, not the management. He had a good eye for smart managers, men like Doug Rose and Roy Rideout, and let them get on with it. Maybe it was The Commander in him: in the navy, the captain of a ship has to rely on the officers and men below him to sail the ship; his job is to keep an eye on them.

If they messed up, he would come down on them. Harry Steele is a polite, civilized man, but his wrath could be fearful if someone working for him failed to perform his duties well, or, even worse, was caught in a lie. This was very seldom a problem, however.

One of the key executives was Roy Rideout. He started at Eastern Provincial Airways as vice-president and eventually became CEO of Clarke Transport. The pool car business was a tough business; it was a high-volume, low-margin business but Roy Rideout took the pool and turned it around, and it became very successful as a contributor to the company.

Clarke had a trucking business in Quebec that was regulated by the province. In the late 1980s, Quebec deregulated the trucking business, which caused some trouble. That was probably the only unsuccessful part of Clarke Transport, a problem in the late 1980s and the early 1990s. NCC got out of the trucking business. There was also a car dealership that came with Clarke, but Harry got rid of that early. He couldn't know that his son Rob would go on to become a success in car dealerships in Atlantic Canada.

Leaving Clarke Transport Behind

In 1997 Harry called for a significant change in direction, deciding that NCC would get out of the transportation business, and become a communications company only, remembers Doug Rose. "I think he decided … the market didn't understand the value under the assets of Newfoundland Capital so the share price was not quite what it should have been. Harry didn't care so much over time because he knew it was cash-flowing money and he was okay, but at the end of the day, he wanted to simplify the business. He saw the returns and the cash flow being concentrated in radio primarily as being the way to go. You know the transportation business is very management intensive; it takes a lot of time, and it's always changing."

On March 25, 1997, the Halterm Income Fund was created. Harry and CN (Canadian National) took the company public through an offering of an income fund, and the guy who did that was Owen Mitchell. Then the Oceanex people took Oceanex public on October 31 of the same year, 1997. Then Clarke issued an IPO on December 9, 1997. So all the assets of the transportation group were being taken public at very high valuations. At the time, income funds were the big thing.

According to Rose, "Steady cash flows and steady dividends [were available], so people paid big multiples for these businesses. I can't remember exact share prices but Halterm was taken public at nine or ten dollars, Oceanex was taken public at nine or ten dollars, and Clarke was around the same level. So these things all went public and, of course, Newfoundland Capital cashed in.

"If you read the annual report on Sedar [a website that carries annual reports of all Canadian publicly listed companies], Harry's address to the shareholders for 1998 talks about the transition and unlocking the underlying value of the assets. He saw an opportunity, I guess, and Owen brought to his attention that all the underlying values of the assets and the cash flow could be freed up and a good multiple earned for them if they were turned into public offerings. So that's what he did."

Roy Rideout was a key manager of Harry Steele's companies for more than twenty years. "Until Harry sold EPA, Clarke was a sister company of EPA. At the time, Clarke was a bit of a holding company; Stanley Clarke in Montreal and his brother Brock owned a bunch of things. One of them was the pool car business, which was the largest part of it … [it] was [involved in] rail freight forwarding from Toronto and Montreal to Vancouver."

Harry Steele had a lot of time for Roy Rideout, and he went on to work in various arms of Clarke Transport. "Harry made me president of Newfoundland Capital so then I had five or six great years of running that, and they were pretty heady days. We gave it lots of shareholder value. Clarke Transport Group was making the most money. We were losing our shirts on the radio.

"Yes, I remember at the board meetings some of the directors wanting to push the radio division off the plank.

"The best money earners would have been Clarke, Oceanex, and Halterm. We were losing in the Quebec trucking operation. I negotiated the sale of the Quebec trucking to Cabano, a Quebec trucker, in the early 1990s. We sold the Quebec trucking and offloaded a lot of red ink there and took a lot of debt off our balance sheet; it was a great transaction. Cabano, of course, has a whole bunch of synergies as it was one of their main competitors in Quebec."

Roy negotiated all the sales of the Clarke Transport units, and eventually left Newfoundland Capital and ran Clarke.

Harry's sense of timing for the sale of Halterm and his other transportation holdings was in retrospect very good and caught the market on the high side at the time. "Harry sold Halterm and Clarke for the same reason. He wanted out of transportation to concentrate on radio and he wanted to unlock shareholder value for NCC," says Doug Rose. "The timing was right because the income fund market for Halterm was hot and the IPO market for Clarke was too so he got good prices for both and maximized his value from these two investments. Business in the port of Halifax was growing and it's always better to sell in a time of growth when a good story can be told. Same for Clarke."

Twelve

The Media Play

Randall, prepare to repel boarders. Mrs. Brown
and I will be at your office at 10:00 a.m.
— Harry Steele

Harry Steele loves newspapers. Reading four or five papers a day was part of his daily routine for years. Politics, business, and stock markets: his three main interests are all well covered in the papers he favours — the *Globe and Mail*, the *Wall Street Journal*, and the *Halifax Chronicle Herald*. He would have loved to have owned the latter paper, but it was not for sale.

Harry and Newfoundland Capital got into the newspaper business in a roundabout way, and through an unlikely partner: an old-fashioned British newsman. David Bentley is a classic British tabloid journalist. Like most of his ilk, he started on a small paper in provincial England then moved up the food chain. He ended up working at the *Northern Echo*, whose editor Harold Evans went on to edit the *Sunday Times*. To further his career, Bentley decided to come to North America for a while; rather than returning to Britain after making his mark here, however, he stayed. David worked for the *Halifax Chronicle Herald* and then the *Financial Post* in Toronto.

When he returned to Nova Scotia from Toronto, he and a partner started the *Sackville News* in Sackville, Nova Scotia, a suburb of Halifax. It was different. A tabloid, not a broad-sheet. It was cheeky, but as David says, there were limits since nothing could approach the style of British tabloids in sedate Nova Scotia.

"It went daily in Sackville, and it sort of lurched to its feet, and then we went to Halifax," says David Bentley. "In Halifax, it was re-named the *Halifax Daily News* [and] competed head to head with the stuffy *Halifax Chronicle Herald*."

"We were a tabloid, so we were quite feisty, and so we covered people and anything that was sensational. Not overly sensational," says David. "There were a lot of families, so you had to be aware of that. The most sensational thing that happened was that Princess Diana showed up and my wife went to an event and spoke to Diana. It was soon after she had got married and she expressed some apprehension at being a princess and how it was difficult. There was a big fuss that we shouldn't have said anything about her, but it sold a lot of papers."

Harry Steele didn't go after Halifax's second paper; it came to him.

The man who did the deal with David was Merv Russell, who at the time was vice-president of acquisitions for Newfoundland Capital and a man with a background in the radio business. "David Bentley and I knew one another, and David and I were having a chat about Harry getting into the radio business because Harry had a very high profile in those days and he asked if he might be interested in the newspaper," says Merv.

"I went to Harry and told him about it, and he said, 'Let's take a run at it.' I said I thought we could only get about 86 percent and Harry said, 'We want the whole damn thing or nothing.' So I put all the pieces together."

David Bentley says Harry made him an offer he couldn't refuse. "In 1985 Harry had just sold the airline and had some money and was just getting his portfolio of other businesses together so he made us an offer for that and we sold it to him," says David.

Rob Steele, who is an admirer of Bentley, sees things a bit differently. The *Halifax Daily News* was his second choice. "My father was interested in the newspaper business; he was trying to buy the [*Halifax*] *Chronicle Herald*, but Graham Dennis wasn't interested in selling, so [Dad] ended up doing a deal buying the *Halifax Daily News* from David Bentley," says Rob.

"The *Halifax Daily News* had the British tabloid style. It went up against the *Chronicle Herald,* which was the established paper. It had a different style, it was a little more saucy, if you will, and it also had the tabloid format versus broadsheet."

In 1997, a dozen years after he bought the *Daily News*, Harry's phone rang, and it was David Radler, Conrad Black's partner in the newspaper business. The two men, along with Peter White, first bought the *Sherbrooke Record* in Quebec in 1968. Radler wanted to know if the *Halifax Daily News* was for sale. By this time, Conrad's newspaper empire had swelled and included the Southam chain with its papers across Canada, the *Daily Telegraph* in London, as well as papers in Australia, the *Chicago Sun-Times*, and even the *Jerusalem Post*. At its peak in 2002, it was the third largest newspaper chain in the English-speaking world, with 450 newspapers and 150 magazines.

Harry must have computed in an instant just why Radler and Black wanted the paper. It would mean a toehold in Atlantic Canada and would give Southam a coast-to-coast reach for national advertisers. Radler asked the price.

"Twenty million," said Harry without missing a beat. Radler didn't balk.

The conversation went on for twenty minutes, half an hour tops, as Radler probed, asking about circulation, market share, and the competition, which he must have known before he made the call.

Rob Steele agrees price wasn't the issue. "Conrad Black and David Radler were trying to build up a national paper network. The *Daily News* was losing money, and Radler called up my father and asked him if he would consider selling the paper. My father said, 'Yeah, I'll consider selling it, but you'll have to chin-up to my price.' Radler asked what the price was and my father replied, 'twenty million' which, quite frankly, made no sense."

At the end of the call, the deal was done: twenty million dollars for a money-losing paper. It proved one thing. Harry Steele knew how to buy, and he knew how to sell. Know when to hold 'em, know when to fold 'em.

"It was a big pass for my father because the paper wasn't making any money," says Rob Steele. "Twenty million. But the buyer's motivation was that he wanted the distribution and to complete the national chain. That's my rationalization why they paid so much."

Conrad Black admired Harry, and he was invited to join the board of Southam, which he did. Being a voracious reader of newspapers, Harry was attracted to owning them, and Rob says he enjoyed the newspaper business, but there was more to it.

"Business for him was the juice, the action. He wasn't married to one particular industry. I don't think he was particularly in love with any of the industries, but then he loved them all. I would say that he probably enjoyed the airline business the most; it was probably a love/hate thing, but that was the watershed for him."

Harry and David Bentley remain friends. "My dealings with Harry were great. You think back in life, and Harry was one of those guys who you knew, and you loved him. He was such an avuncular, nice guy … you could call on at any time and ask him anything and he did the right things," says David.

Community Newspapers

About the same time as he bought the *Halifax Daily News*, Harry and Newfoundland Capital picked up Robinson Blackmore, a commercial printing business in Newfoundland and the Maritime provinces that also owned a string of community newspapers in Newfoundland.

"Robinson Blackmore was near and dear to his heart because he bought it from the three guys who had bought it from Andrew Crosbie," says Doug Rose, who worked with Harry for many years.

"Harry loved the community newspaper business in Newfoundland, and Robinson Blackmore was a big asset for him and a very good earner. The guy who ran Robinson Blackmore was Doyle Roberts," says Doug. "He and I would be two of the guys out and about looking for acquisitions and smaller community newspapers in Atlantic Canada. The concept was to have a 'centre of gravity' or something like that, a centre where you could consolidate all the printing and then add papers on to it. The printing press had lots of capacity, and you could buy papers up and add them on and consolidate your overheads."

Though the advent of the internet hurt big city newspapers, small community papers were somewhat immune. Like local radio stations, they were an excellent way for local advertisers to target their audience.

Harry also bought some specialty publications in Ontario. His financial guru Ivan Kilpatrick had retired to Simcoe, Ontario, and he spotted a group of newspapers based in Tillsonburg, Ontario, and a group of specialty publications in nearby Delhi.

"They did specialty publications for firemen and groups like that, but they had a group of community newspapers. Harry bought that based primarily on Ivan's recommendation. It was eventually sold off in 1997 and one of the guys who used to work for Harry, Mike Fredericks, bought it," says Doug Rose.

Robinson Blackmore stayed in Harry's stable longer. It became the largest commercial printer in Atlantic Canada.

Printing and Publishing in Atlantic Canada

Commercial Printing, Corner Brook, Newfoundland
Print Atlantic, Dartmouth, Nova Scotia
Print Atlantic, Fredericton, New Brunswick

Print Atlantic, Moncton, New Brunswick
Robinson Blackmore, St. John's, Newfoundland
Robinson Blackmore, Grand Falls, Newfoundland

The Advertiser, Grand Falls, Newfoundland
The Aurora, Labrador City, Newfoundland
The Beacon, Gander, Newfoundland
The Charter, Jerseyside, Newfoundland
The Coaster, Harbour Breton, Newfoundland
The Compass, Carbonear, Newfoundland
The Express, St. John's, Newfoundland
The Georgian, Stephenville, Newfoundland
The Gulf News, Channel-Port Aux Basques, Newfoundland
The Humber Log, Corner Brook, Newfoundland
The Labradorian, Happy Valley, Newfoundland
The Nor'Wester, Springdale, Newfoundland
The Packet, Clarenville, Newfoundland
The Pilot, Lewisporte, Newfoundland
The Southern Gazette, Marystown, Newfoundland
Voisey's Bay News, St. John's, Newfoundland

Radio

It all started with a 1,100-watt radio station in Charlottetown. By the time Harry bought CHTN in 1985, it had bumped up its power to 10,000 watts. It was the first of many that he would buy.

Newfoundland Capital Corporation ended up as a pure radio play. In the radio biz, it is known as Newcap Radio, a much snappier name in a business far away from trucks, ferries, and container terminals. When it was sold for $508 million in 2018, it owned 101 radio licences across Canada.

No one could have guessed Newfoundland Capital would one day become a media giant.

"Ivan Kilpatrick was extremely important to my father because he was a counter-balance for his weaknesses, which he recognized, and that's why Ivan was so good for him," says Rob Steele. "Ivan was smart, articulate, a good finance man, and he was a guy who was happy to be in a support role to support my father as the entrepreneur. Ivan himself was not the entrepreneur type, but he recognized talents and drive in entrepreneurs."

As mentioned earlier, Ivan was an academic who knew the theory of business. And as also mentioned, he was a man who preferred things you could touch, rather than ephemeral businesses like radio. And it would appear he did not care too much for the people in the radio business. That cut both ways.

"He was always very nice, but he had a bit of a Jekyll and Hyde in him," says Rob Steele. "You should probably talk to guys like Merv Russell, who was his VP of marketing at the airline. Merv is the reason that Newcap is in the radio business."

Back to the beginning. Merv Russell met Harry Steele when the radio executive, then living in Toronto, was a guest speaker at an event in St. Andrews by-the-Sea in New Brunswick. Harry spoke to him after the meeting and said he was interested in getting into the radio business. They kept in touch, and later Merv was invited to the launch of the Eastern Provincial Airways service to Toronto. Next thing he knew, he was working for Harry.

"Harry said he had a number of issues in the airline and he wanted me to come over and have a look at [things]," says Merv. "I ended up leaving the corner of Wellesley and Bay in Toronto and ending up in The Albatross Hotel in Gander in the airline business with Harry. He was still zeroing in on wanting to be in the radio business and newspapers."

While they waited for that opportunity to present itself, Merv became vice-president of marketing at EPA, a job Harry once had. After Harry sold EPA, Merv became vice-president of acquisitions for Newfoundland Capital Corporation.

One of his tasks was to get into the radio business. He and Harry had tried to buy something in Newfoundland but were turned down by the CRTC (Canadian Radio-television and Telecommunications Commission). Then opportunity appeared under their noses.

"There was a guy on the NCC board by the name of Alan Scales, a partner at a big law firm here in Atlantic Canada. Scales was a part owner of a radio station at the time in Charlottetown, CHTN. So I asked Alan what was going on in the radio business and he said it was the stupidest money-losing deal he had ever been involved in," recalls Merv. "I asked 'Why don't you get rid of it?' He asked, 'Who would be interested in it, you?' I said, 'No, but Harry is.' So he said, 'Let's have a chat.' So, at the Citadel Inn, after the meeting, we all agreed that we should go and have a look at it. Within three or four days, I was in the car going to the Bank of Nova Scotia in Charlottetown and taking over the loan."

The sale price was one dollar, and Newfoundland Capital took over the $134,000 bank loan. Everyone was happy — well, almost everyone. Alan Scales was probably licking his wounds on the loss of his original investment.

Merv went after another radio station, CKDH in Amherst, Nova Scotia. "We cut a deal in a room at the Wandlyn Motel. I lived four doors from Harry here in Dartmouth, and I went in, and I said, 'We got it.' Harry picked up the phone and called his brother-in-law who lived in Sackville, which is the next town to Amherst, and we regaled each other discussing the deal.

"Then we had to put together the presentation to the acquisition committee, which was made up of five people. A guy named Henry Taylor did most of the work on that, and we went into the committee without Harry, who wasn't there that day, October 22, 1984, and we made the presentation, and it was turned down.

"They were all bean-counters, and Harry wasn't there. They said 'No, no, this radio stuff and media stuff is moving too fast.'

"I said that was the reason I was brought here. I was told you wanted to be in the radio business. Kilpatrick, and I'll never forget him as long as I live, came outside the office and took his stubby finger and pointed it at my nose and said, 'If you think Newfoundland Capital is going to become a pure radio play, you're in the wrong place.' I said, 'Okay,' and then thirty days later I left."

Eventually, Newfoundland Capital Corporation did become a pure media play. Merv Russell says he reminded Harry of the incident a few times. Merv went on to build a competing radio network of his own.

Harry's long-time banker, Randall Hartlen of the Bank of Nova Scotia, was a bit surprised when Newfoundland Capital made its big move into radio. "He explained it to me saying, 'Randy, it's a great business. You reach a certain point where every dollar that comes in the top dribbles right down to the bottom.' And that's how the radio business does work. You have a certain cost base and if you generate enough ad revenue it literally does flow straight down."

Scott Weatherby joined Newfoundland Capital Corporation as chief financial officer in 2000, just as the company was starting the transition to radio. Scott was born in Tatamagouche, Nova Scotia, in the northern part of the province, just north of Truro. A chartered accountant, he worked for the accounting firm Grant Thornton for ten years before joining Newfoundland Capital. As soon as he came on board, he noticed the change in culture from an accounting firm to a business headed by entrepreneurs.

"At the CA [chartered accounting] firm, I was looking at multiple different companies doing a wide variety of work, but here [Newfoundland Capital] you are able to focus on one business, and the big thing for me, personally, was that I was able to invest the time in the business. When you're working in a CA firm, productivity is always by hour, so you can only invest a certain number of hours with every client you have, so it was nice not to have to worry about tracking my time and billing out my time and just focusing on what's important," says Scott.

"However, the core training of spending the majority of your time on the most … where you get the most return or the most reward, is the same. I thought it was ironic that it was a completely different business but you did have to concentrate on what gives you the best return and you get that discipline at a CA firm and you bring that discipline when you're running a business."

Scott worked with Harry and Rob getting rid of what he referred to as "nuisance businesses" — things that took up a lot of time but didn't make a lot of money.

"There were investments in internet-streaming radio and he was involved in some electronics companies, you name it. Rob quickly realized that all these extracurricular companies were just consuming way too much time and we should focus on a core business. We had to pick a core business and at the time radio seemed to be the right one and hindsight has proven that it was the right way to go," says Scott.

"We proceeded to sell all these companies that were a distraction, and then we went on to sell the printing and publishing, which was a good cash-flow producer at the time but we could see that it was going to be capital intensive. So, it made sense for us to divest of that and pour the funds into radio because radio has a much lower capital requirement and higher cash flow. It was just a stronger business. So, once we divested of the printing and publishing in 2002 and were able to focus on radio; it really allowed it to grow exponentially over the years up until the point where we sold it."

One of the things that excited Scott was that NCC owned the radio station he listened to as a teenager growing up in Halifax. "Q104, CFRQ, was launched back in the mid-1980s when I was in my teens and it was rock music, which I enjoyed. Upstairs in our house we could just barely get it, and I always found it ironic that fifteen years later I was working for this company that owned my favourite radio station when I was growing up," says Scott.

Thirteen

Cleaning House:
Corporate Re-organization

You can't save your way to prosperity.
— Harry Steele

The revolutionary change at Newfoundland Capital Corporation came in 1997. The company sold off all its transportation assets, spinning them into income trusts, and sold almost all the print assets.

Harry Steele re-invented himself again, this time as a media mogul, controlling radio stations.

The radio adventure started debt-free. This is how the changes were explained to shareholders in the 1998 annual report:

> [Nineteen ninety-seven] was the best year ever for Newfoundland Capital Corporation Limited (NCC). On consolidated revenue of $289.7 million, the Company made a record net operating profit of $7.4 million, before gains on dispositions. Corresponding cash flow from operations was $17.3 million, also a record.
>
> WE DECIDED TO REALIZE SOME OF THE UNDERLYING VALUE OF NCC'S ASSETS FOR THE BENEFIT OF ITS SHAREHOLDERS.

Of even more significance, however, was the decision to realize some of the underlying value of NCC's assets for the benefit of its shareholders. This value had long existed but had never been fully recognized by the market. During 1997, the Company divested its interest in several transportation and publishing ventures for an after-tax profit of $36.2 million. This boosted net income to $43.6 million or $3.88 per share. Sold during the year were the Company's interests in Halterm, Oceanex, the *Halifax Daily News,* and NCC Publishing, as well as a number of smaller operations. Proceeds from the dispositions, along with the cash flow from operations, were used to pay down the debt. By year-end, a total of $42.6 million had been retired, leaving the Company essentially debt free.

Further, the remaining transportation holdings were sold to the public during the first quarter of 1998, raising $92 million. This yielded an after-tax gain of approximately $30 million to $35 million. The Clarke operations sold through this public offering were, on a combined basis, the largest segment of NCC's overall business. Last year they accounted for $208 million (72 percent) of the Company's total revenue and $8.5 million (54 percent) of its operating income, before interest and taxes.

All of these events, which represent a significant transformation of your Company, have culminated in a very positive result for the shareholders. For some time, the market had made it clear that as long as these assets remained under the conglomerate umbrella of NCC, the Company's shares would remain undervalued. By separating these operations, it was our hope that they would be more fairly valued in the marketplace, and they were. The price for a

Class A Subordinate Voting Share of NCC rose from $3.10 on December 31, 1996, to $11.35 at the time of writing. The market capitalization of the Company has grown from $35 million at the end of 1996 to its current level of $130 million.

NCC's approach has always been to buy strong, reasonably priced operating companies and add value through redirection or expansion. There is no doubt that there is yet more value to be added to the group of companies we have just sold. We are confident that the new owners and the employees of these businesses will benefit from that potential.

AT YEAR-END, THE COMPANY HAD VIRTUALLY NO DEBT.

Of even greater importance is how confident we are about the future of NCC. At year-end, the Company had virtually no debt and a cash balance of $0.9 million, which will grow by $27.0 million with proceeds from instalment receipts related to the earlier sale of Halterm and Oceanex. In addition to this, our cash position will be significantly enhanced by the receipt of $92 million in proceeds from the sale of Clarke. These proceeds will be received partly in 1998, with the balance forthcoming in the first quarter of 1999. After payment of all related income taxes, NCC will have a cash position of approximately $78 million. Combined with profitable ongoing operations in radio and publishing, this strong financial position makes for a very promising and rewarding future. The NCC of today is no longer a conglomerate. It is a more clearly focused communications company. As the feature segment of this year's annual report demonstrates, we are clearly intent on building our future primarily around the radio business.

WE ARE CLEARLY INTENT ON BUILDING OUR FUTURE PRIMARILY AROUND THE RADIO BUSINESS.

The Canadian Radio-television and Telecommunications Commission (CRTC) is widely expected to begin deregulating the Canadian radio industry in the spring of 1998. With this deregulation comes the opportunity to add substantial shareholder value. As an example, following the 1992 deregulation of radio in the United States, radio cash flow valuation multiples almost doubled. Obviously, there is great upside potential for radio in Canada.

Substantial progress has been made in our Radio Division over the past year. Operating profit, before interest and taxes, increased by 66 percent in 1997 to $2.4 million. This was achieved on a modest 3 percent increase in total revenue, which stood at $19.3 million for the year. Operating cash flow increased to $3.7 million in 1997, up 27 percent over the previous year.

There were some disappointments in radio during the year. Our application to the CRTC to acquire an AM/FM station in Saint John was withdrawn, and an application for a Toronto FM frequency was denied and awarded to the CBC.

On the positive side, we expanded our interest in CJMO-FM in Moncton by acquiring an additional 12.6 percent, bringing our ownership to 62.2 percent. Further, during the first quarter of 1998, our existing local management agreement in Halifax entered into a partnership with a successful AM/FM combination owned by CHUM Limited.

In addition to our radio properties, the Company will continue to operate the publishing business of Robinson Blackmore (RB) in Newfoundland. RB operates a group of seventeen newspaper publications and is Atlantic Canada's largest commercial printer. Last year was particularly good for RB, which has been a stable earnings and cash flow contributor for the past thirteen years. The operation benefited from substantial advertising and printing activity associated with the Cabot 500 celebrations, a federal election, and a provincial education referendum. With economists predicting that the Newfoundland economy will outperform the rest of Canada, 1998 should be another excellent year for RB.

WE HAVE TRANSFORMED NEWFOUNDLAND CAPITAL INTO A MORE CLEARLY FOCUSED COMMUNICATIONS COMPANY.

While it took only one year to realize the underlying value of the Company's transportation assets, it should be remembered that this value was not created overnight. It was built by the hard work and dedication of many people over the years. We would like to thank all the employees who have been part of the total company.

We also extend our deep appreciation to members of our Board of Directors who will be stepping down. Robert Bandeen, Rowland Frazee, Hubert Marleau, and David Matheson have served our Company with distinction over the years. Their contribution has been a significant factor in our success. A special word of thanks goes to Roy Rideout, who has been President and Chief Operating Officer since 1993 and a Director since 1994. Roy is leaving his position to become Chairman and Chief Executive Officer of Clarke upon closing of the public offering. I believe that Clarke will continue to be a great company under his leadership.

All of us at Newfoundland Capital look forward to the future with great expectations and excitement.

(signed) Harry R. Steele
Harry R. Steele
Chairman and Chief Executive Officer
March 5, 1998

Newfoundland Capital Corporation Limited

ANNUAL   REPORT   1981

Newfoundland Capital Corporation logo on an annual report.

These are the detailed reasons the company outlined for the roll of the dice move into radio, though it is hard to imagine Harry in person waxing lyrical about the wonders of good time oldies:

Stay tuned for the rise of radio.

Not since the introduction of FM in the late 1960s have the prospects for Radio been so bright. After years of lacklustre advertising revenue and declining market share, Canada's once-beleaguered radio industry is beginning to show signs of life. And Newfoundland Capital's Radio Division is ready to capitalize on the industry's return to profitability.

The company's turnaround in radio has been achieved by sticking to three basic strategies. First, the company has been steadily improving the market share of its radio properties by focusing programming on specific demographic markets. Second, through the application of digital technology, the company has been able to improve program quality while lowering operating costs.

And finally, by the use of local management agreements, the Company has been able to share administrative, marketing and engineering costs with competitors, creating economies of scale that dramatically improve the profitability of its stations.

What's more, prospects for the Company's radio properties, and the industry at large are getting better. In the spring of 1998, the Canadian Radio-television and Telecommunications Commission (CRTC) is widely expected to at least double the number of radio stations that a company may own in a given market. The impact on the value and profitability of Canadian radio properties is expected to be dramatic.

Below are the radio stations NCC owned by early 1998. When the company sold its assets twenty years later in 2018, there were 101 radio licences worth $508 million. By that measure, the move into radio was inspired.

Nova Scotia
In Halifax, KIXX-AM plays "Continuous Country Hits" and Q104-FM is the only classic rock station.

New Brunswick
C103-FM, serving Moncton, southern New Brunswick, and northern Nova Scotia, plays an adult contemporary format and continues to be #1 with the 18–54 age group.

Prince Edward Island
CHTN-AM, 720 on the dial, broadcasts "Good Time Oldies."

Newfoundland
The KIXX Country Network includes five stations. CKIX and CKXX are Newfoundland's only country FM stations while CKXD-AM, CKXG-AM, and CKXB-AM serve markets in Gander, Grand Falls-Windsor, and Musgravetown, respectively. CJYQ-AM in St. John's features a "Classic Hits" format.

Ontario
CJLB-FM, at 105.3 on the dial, broadcasts a country format to Thunder Bay and surrounding area.

Alberta
CFCW-AM and MIX 96-FM are strong performers in the Edmonton market. CFCW is all country while MIX96 targets adult contemporary listeners.

Corporate portrait of Harry Steele.

A paragraph in the 1999 annual report summarized what had been sold:

> The sale of Clarke in an initial public offering on March 17, 1998, completed the transformation of Newfoundland Capital Corporation from a conglomerate to a focused communications company. The divestiture of the Transportation Group and certain underperforming publishing operations began in late 1996 with the sale of Southwestern Ontario Printing and Publishing. It continued in 1997 with the sale

of the Company's interests in Halterm and Oceanex to income trusts. Other publishing assets, including the *Halifax Daily News*, NCC Publishing, and NCC Specialty Publications, were sold privately in 1997 and early 1998.

Roy Rideout, who was CEO of Clark Transport, was part of the team that spun off the various assets. "It was at a time when multiples were great, and IPO's were flying out the door, so there was a window of opportunity for Harry to simplify things because we had always been concerned about our multiple. I mean what was NCC? Was it a transportation company or a communications company or what? We were suffering from the fact that the communications assets were trading at higher multiples than the transportation and the transportation was trading at higher multiples than the 'holding companies' like Newfoundland Capital.* We were trying to figure out how to do that because we were losing shareholder value there.** So then this opportunity came along, and the first one out the door was Halterm in 1996, and it went out as an income trust.

"We went on the road show, where I had the unpleasant task of firing the president of Halterm and brought in this other guy, Patrick Morin, and he's the guy who did the road show with me. We extracted some pretty good coin for that; the lead on that was First Marathon, Lawrence Bloomberg. So, we got that one out the door at upward of a hundred million or something like that. Of course, with Halterm, our co-owners were CN, so we had to split the proceeds with them at about a 75/25 split because we had a management contract and we were taking more out of Halterm than they were and they recognized that. So, we ended up getting pretty good coin out of that.

---

* A multiple measures the price of the stock against profit and earnings. Older industries usually have low multiples; more exciting or speculative stocks have higher multiples.

** Shareholder value is business jargon for the stock price.

"Then it was Oceanex and, of course, with them we had four partners: Fednav, CSL, and so on, and I remember meeting with the lads from the other companies at the dining room at the Queen E to acquaint them with the notion of selling Oceanex, again, into another income trust, and when the numbers were presented to them they all agreed to do it and that was another road show.

"Well, the two members on the board from NCC were Harry and I, and from Fednav John Peacock and a gentleman from CSL. That would have been in 1997, and then Clarke was next, and it was the largest; by then we had evolved into a container operation.

"Halterm was quite separate from Clarke, which was involved in the overland, and we had evolved a little bit from the box-car operation to part boxcar and part container. We had also set up a trucking operation based in Halifax which was growing in leaps and bounds as well. So, the Clarke part of it was the most significant piece of the whole puzzle, and I went with it because there wouldn't be anything left except a small radio division, so I became the first CEO of Clarke, and that was in 1998.

"As soon as the IPO was complete, I left as president of NCC and became CEO of Clarke, and I relocated to Toronto. Then, of course, Harry and I parted company again, and as I have often said to him over the years, he sold me twice: he sold me from the airline, and he sold me from Clarke. But even though our trails parted again, I [have] kept in pretty close contact with him to this day.

"The move into radio was not a big money maker at the start. Harry knew he needed managers who knew the radio business, but the type of person who thrives in the world of radio might not be the type who is popular with The Commander.

"We hired a guy, Bob Templeton, a good radio guy, to come in and turn over some of the stones. He and Harry never really got along, but Bob was the guy who turned the radio division from red to black. He just knew the business. He was a great believer in consumer research and changing formats as necessary [to improve] ratings to attract the advertisers. We saw him turn it around and saw that he was pretty savvy, so we started buying radio stations. We would have done even better if we had jumped on a couple of opportunities that he had recommended back in the mid-1990s.

"There was a Toronto station that came up that was tremendously expensive, and it had no ratings at all; it was like 1 percent or 2 percent of the market or something like that. All I remember is that we had said no and that was a mistake. Bob was a guy who was very expansion-minded and very growth-minded. He was turning around the St. John's operation, which was losing money, and he turned it into a big cash cow.

"Because he has a lot of the military in him, Harry wants people on deck first thing in the morning, and he doesn't like smokers, and [Bob] was one of these guys who really didn't get started until about 9:30 in the morning and smoked like a chimney."

The Commander and the radio guru parted ways. That is the kind of behind the scenes corporate drama that does not make it into the annual report. Instead, the report summed up what had been sold and emphasized that the company was now a radio play.

Newfoundland Capital decided to keep a small slice of print media, mainly the community papers and Robinson Blackmore, at the time the largest commercial printer in the Atlantic provinces. As the 1998 annual report stated, things such as elections and the oil boom in Newfoundland meant customers were buying a lot of ink:

Publishing

Publishing contribution increased by $0.9 million during the year. The decision to dispose of underperforming properties left only Robinson Blackmore and NCC Specialty Publications at year-end. Adjusting for dispositions in 1997, contribution was up by $1.3

million on revenue improvement of 8.5 percent or $2.0 million.

The major reason for the improvement was that last year's losses at NCC Specialty Publications were all but eliminated. In Newfoundland, Robinson Blackmore benefited from a federal election, the education referendum, and the Cabot 500 celebrations. Economic forecasts indicate that Newfoundland will enjoy one of the highest growth rates in the country in 1998. With Hibernia in production, the Voisey's Bay nickel discovery and numerous other opportunities underway, the economic future for Newfoundland has never looked better.

By 1999 the company called itself "a communications company engaged in Radio and Publishing and Printing. The company operates fourteen radio licences across Canada and publishes twenty community newspaper and magazine publications."

The strategy was finally paying off. Income from continuing operations was up sharply, and earnings per share at twenty-seven cents was up 60 percent from two years earlier, when the radio plan really kicked in. And all this from radio stations, assets that were less capital intensive — meaning they took less money to run — than things like shipping terminals and trucks.

The company continued to be frustrated in its ambitions to land a station in the rich Toronto market. Harry Steele's note to shareholders said the price was "beyond what we were prepared to pay." That reinforces Roy Rideout's earlier comments that Harry made a mistake not stepping up to the plate to pay for a Toronto licence.

In the company report dated March 1, 2000, Harry R. Steele, chairman and chief executive officer of Newfoundland Capital Corporation signed off his comments in a very informal way, in a sentence he probably wrote himself: "We have just completed our first full year without Transportation. It's nice."

By the next year, The Commander reported that there were twenty-five radio stations in the stable, including VOCM of St. John's, a radio station Harry would have listened to as a boy. It also was granted a new FM licence in Moncton, New Brunswick, something the company predicted it would do a few years earlier.

The other news was the expansion of the printing business, which picked up two new firms and installed a "heat-web" press in Halifax, a machine that dries the ink faster, increasing productivity.

Newfoundland Capital ushered in the new millennium with thirty-seven radio licences, including nineteen in Alberta, one of which was a jazz FM station in the rich Calgary market. The company was also awarded an FM licence in Ottawa, which it pointed out was the third largest English radio market in Canada. All that meant shelling out boatloads of cash — $40 million just for the Alberta properties.

It was during this period that Harry, and his wife, Catherine, thought about slowing down, if only slightly. "He started to pull back a little beforehand, we had that succession issue, and we were trying to figure out who should run it, and we made the call for Rob to do it," says John Steele. "Dad was the guy who realized that he had to pull back and let Rob do his thing. Rob was the right choice then, and I think he has delivered in spades."

Rob Steele came aboard as president and chief operating officer in 2001. Although you might think that Rob's decision to move to NCC was a natural one, in fact, the decision to join the company was made only after some lively debate. This was another drama that couldn't go into the annual report, as Rob Steele had to be talked into joining his father.

"I went on an alternate career path of car dealerships. Along with two other guys, I bought my first dealership when I was twenty-eight. I was the third partner in a dealership called Collins

Chrysler. Before that, I had the *Auto Trader* in Newfoundland. I had sold that and I was looking for something to do, and I found out that this guy was looking to sell, so I ended up partnering with him. That's how I got into the car business.

"My father was always trying to woo me over to work with him, but I never particularly wanted to do that. One Christmas — I was thirty-nine at the time — he came to me. He was at his home in Clearwater, Florida, and I happened to be in Miami between Christmas and New Year's and my father and mother drove to Miami. Unbeknownst to me, my father and mother had an idea.

"My mother had sat down with my father and asked me to come over to NCC and run the company because he wanted to step back. Even though I had been on the board since 1995, I was never particularly enthralled with or impressed with the way Newfoundland Capital was run. I always thought it was direction-less because it was a conglomerate comprised of many different businesses, from ferry terminals to trucking to newspapers to radio — a bunch of stuff in different sectors, different industries. The [stock] market had a hard time valuing the stock because it was a conglomerate; nowadays valuations are predicated on what the industry or sector is. If it's media companies or radio, it trades at multiples of revenue or whatever. The idea of being a conglom-erate works better privately than publicly for that reason.

"On top of that, [there was the operational style of the com-pany], and my father and I had talked about this over the years. His strength was more in buying and selling companies [but he didn't always stick to that]. If there was a fault in my father's style, he was a little too domineering, and he didn't give people free rein to operate. So, he had this company, and he was great at buying and selling businesses. He can smell value, and he's good at selling and monetizing the value of those assets. But in between operating them and turning them around, he has a mixed record.

"When he came to talk to me, I initially turned it down. I just wasn't interested, because: one, I didn't particularly like the management team he had in place; and, on top of that, I was thirty-nine years old and had seven or eight car dealerships, and I was on a bit of a tear. I had things rolling pretty well, and I was the master of my own ship in a private company that I owned. For me to go over and run NCC as a public company, which we owned 36 percent of the equity at that time, meant I would have to play the public market game, and, on top of that, deal with the rebuild of the management team. It didn't appear attractive to me, so I said no.

"My folks stayed with me a couple of days, and they both talked to me about it, and, unbeknownst to me, my brothers had already been told about it, and they endorsed it, and they wanted me to do it. Over those couple of days and ensuing weeks, I thought about it, and I became intrigued with it, and I said, 'Maybe I can, maybe I should do this, maybe this is a good opportunity.' But in my view, we needed to reshape the company a little bit and get it more single-focused.

"So, I talked to my father over this period, and I said, 'Okay, how about this: If I do this, you'll have to let me run this company as I see fit. If you think that I'm headed for a cliff, you can hold on to my collar.' He said, 'That's fine, do what you want with it.' He was used to buying and selling stuff anyway. The other caveat was that I had to hire my own management team. He said, 'Who are you thinking, what do you mean?'"

Rob then described how he went about running the corporation the way he wanted. That meant getting rid of some people, in particular managers who had been close to his father. One of them made the mistake of calling Rob to congratulate him on his appointment, but was cheeky enough to say he had wanted the top job but "You're the son."

The icing on the cake. That manager was soon gone.

The board of Newfoundland Capital. (l-r) Donald Warr, Michael (Mickey) MacDonald, Robert G. Steele, David T. Matheson, Harry R. Steele, Alan S. MacPhee, and John R. Steele.

The man was shocked and had to sit down. No one on the board knew about this, including the chairman, Harry Steele. That night Rob broke it to him.

"My father was definitely not happy about it, and he had me in the penalty box for a long period of time, but it was the right move; it worked.

"Radio is where I wanted to go because radio had good margins, it is an attractive business, and I think we had fourteen radio stations at the time. I just wanted to divest of all this other stuff, and I sold off all the newspapers. We tried an IPO, and we tried to sell it to Transcontinental. We ended up trying to do an

IPO separately and then about three or four months later I did the deal with Transcontinental, with the owner of the company, Remi Marcoux.

"My plan was to get rid of all the stuff that was capital intensive, wasn't attractive, and didn't have a future. We wrote off a bunch of junk that someone convinced my father to get, like Millennial Money and some internet stuff. I wanted to clean up the organization and get it focused and start trying to develop radio expertise and managers and that kind of thing. That's why we became a broadcast company."

The corporate re-organization was complete.

Stingray first approached Newfoundland Capital Corporation about buying the firm in the spring of 2017. The timing wasn't right, but Stingray and its president and CEO, Eric Boyko, came back a year later. Then everything happened very quickly. His mission was to seal the deal in ten days. That was around April 20 of 2018, when there was a lunch meeting at the Prince George restaurant in Halifax followed by further talks at the Bicycle Thief restaurant on Lower Water Street.

"The timing wasn't right for them when they first approached us. They didn't really have everything lined up, like financing, and they weren't ready, even though they thought they were," says Scott Weatherby. "We went along with our business, [thinking] that they might come back someday or they may not but they did come back in late April. The mission of the president and CEO of Stingray was to get this done in ten days and they basically did it."

Everything was agreed to and a public announcement made on May 2, 2018. Then came the paperwork. "It was extremely complex," says Scott Weatherby. The deal finally closed in November of 2018.

Newcap, as it called itself publicly, ended its life with 101 radio licences across Canada. A far cry from the transportation conglomerate, with a lot of other businesses thrown in. The price paid by Stingray for the firm was $508 million, a testament to Harry Steele's entrepreneurial spirit and Rob Steele's single-minded re-org. As Scott Weatherby remarked after the sale, "Both Mr. Steele and Rob are entrepreneurs to the nth degree, never standing still, always being creative and always motivated to do something."

Fourteen

Craig Dobbin

The path he followed was one uniquely carved by himself.
— Harry Steele at Craig Dobbin's funeral

Harry Steele and Craig Dobbin were like chalk and cheese. "Two more different people you would never find," says Craig's widow, Elaine.

Maybe that's not quite true; they did have a few things in common. Both were Newfoundlanders, born in poverty, and each made a huge success of their lives as successful entrepreneurs. Harry, as has been mentioned, was born in the remote outport of Musgrave Harbour. Craig Dobbin was born in The Battery, a district of St. John's and one of the poorest places in the city. Like Harry, he was always proud of his roots, no matter how rich he became. Also, the two men loved the wilderness and salmon fishing on the isolated rivers of Labrador. And the two titans of Newfoundland business, self-made men, admired each other and were the best of friends.

Aside from those shared things, Craig Dobbin and Harry Steele could hardly have been more different. Steele, by his own description, is frugal. Craig Dobbin, by general consensus, was flamboyant. Harry avoids the limelight, Craig thrived in it. Harry drives a seven-year-old Chrysler, Craig Dobbin once spent $600,000 on a Rolls Royce that accumulated barely seven thousand kilometres before being sold for a third of its original cost. It is unlikely that any two businessmen in Canada were so closely linked through the heights of their careers.

Craig and Harry were close friends even though they were different in their personalities. Harry grew up in a pretty frugal environment when he was younger; later, when he had some money, he was willing to spend money but he had to know where it went and what it was for. Craig, on the other hand, was a little more cavalier in his spending and risk-taking, but they remained loyal friends right until his death.

"Craig Dobbin was a different guy. He was an intuitive man who had no fear. His success came about through a unique combination of balls and charm," says Peter Steele. "My father and he connected over salmon fishing, but they really also connected over their restless spirits and putting the spirits at peace in both of their favourite place in the world which was the big land of Labrador. Their friendship knew no bounds, and their loyalty to each other knew no end. Craig, in a business sense, was my father's alter ego. Both of them embraced risk/reward in their own calculated way to the level of their personalities and ambition. But Craig was a swashbuckling entrepreneur of huge success who had no fear and who my father deeply enjoyed both his company and friendship."

"Harry had such a regard for Dobbin. He was, I think, his deepest friend. When Dobbin died, I went with Harry to the funeral, and that was a major moment in his life," says Rex Murphy. "Those two were a pair, even though Dobbin's personality was the opposite of Harry's, and vice versa. He admired the kind of buccaneer, reckless entrepreneur, though they were both self-made men."

They were certainly different men when it came to business. Craig Dobbin was a risk taker. So was Harry Steele at the start of his career, with Eastern Provincial Airways, but most of his decisions were calculated. He was an astute student of markets and knew an opportunity when he saw it. Craig Dobbin was a brilliant entrepreneur, but his risk-taking was more seat of the pants stuff. If he had a gut feel for something, he went for it.

"Craig Dobbin was my father's closest friend [but] I think they were polar opposites in terms of lifestyle," says Rob Steele. "My father, I think, lived vicariously through Craig Dobbin. My father was always a measured, controlled guy who didn't have extra-curricular habits that sort of wouldn't lend themselves well to business. Craig was the true swashbuckler entrepreneur that saw no walls that he couldn't break through. I think he and my father had that in common, but my father certainly was lifted, inspired by Craig."

John Steele agrees that Craig and his father had an "incredibly close" relationship, even though he, too, describes them as polar opposites: "I think Dad lived vicariously through Dobbin. Dobbin could do anything — whether or not he had the money he would do it. Nothing was too big for him and Dad liked the energy he got from Craig. They both came from nothing, and they were self-made guys and both patriotic Newfoundlanders. So where Dad lived vicariously through Dobbin, I think Dobbin used Dad as a sounding board to keep him focused and reel him in and grounded a bit," says John. "Craig was a glass half-full guy. He had real charisma and a real ability to keep current and in tune with the now and what was happening. The world was his oyster. He was an incredibly generous guy."

"Craig loved Harry and Harry obviously loved Craig. It was a relationship that few would understand," says Elaine. "Harry is ultra-conservative and does everything very quietly, and my husband was very flamboyant and didn't do anything quietly. Craig loved to entertain, and Harry despised it."

Despite their differences, Harry was one of the few people Craig listened to, according to Elaine. "Craig had the highest admiration and respect for Harry Steele. There weren't many other people that he would confide in or take advice from as the way he did Harry," says Elaine. "They would see each other whenever they could, but I can assure you of one thing: the two of them spoke almost every day on the phone even if they were travelling.

"If Harry told him something was too risky [or] impulsive, Craig would back down. No one else could tell him what to do."

In his biography of Craig Dobbin, *One Hell of Ride*, the author John Lawrence Reynolds notes: "As he did on almost every major business decision, Dobbin conferred with Harry Steele."

Reynolds details how the two men met. The folklore is that it was on a salmon river, but it happened while Harry was still in the navy:

> Back in 1969, Dobbin had learned that the Canadian Armed Forces were planning to build sixty houses to accommodate members of the armed forces and their families at Gander. With many of his CMHC-funded apartments in the region sitting empty, Dobbin arranged a meeting with the base commander to pitch the flats as an economical alternative.
>
> After listening to his pitch, the commander raised his eyebrows and told Dobbin he knew about the apartments. "They were so damned cramped," the commander noted, that residing in them would be "like living inside a Salvation Army drum." Dobbin roared with laughter at the description and spent the rest of the day in the commander's company trading stories and discussing business and politics. He never gained a lease from his pitch, but he acquired Commander Harry Steele as a lifelong pal.
>
> Steele served as [Dobbin's] confidante, mentor, ally, and comrade in the years that followed, though it is almost impossible to imagine two more contrasting personalities.

Three amigos (l-r): Craig Dobbin, Harry Steele, and Austin Garrett, a close friend of Harry's.

Their relationship was cemented in 1980 when Dobbin became involved in a quest for investment money. That year Steele was contacted by Allan Bristow, a former Royal Navy helicopter pilot who had launched a helicopter service dubbed "Air Whaling Limited," renamed Bristow Helicopters several years later. The firm, located in Surrey, England, was a major participant in the United Kingdom's offshore petroleum industry, primarily in the North Sea. With activity stirring in Newfoundland, Bristow saw the opportunity to expand into the North American market. Knowing Harry Steele's business success and military background, Bristow approached Steele with a direct offer: "We have similar backgrounds," Bristow said in a telephone call. "We are both former naval officers, and I want you to be my partner in opening a helicopter service over there."

At the time, Harry was on the board of Okanagan Helicopters. Reynolds describes the scene: "[With the] opening in the province's offshore oil industry, Okanagan, the country's largest helicopter service firm, made a pitch to service the first producing well in the Hibernia field. [Bristow wanted to do the same thing.]

Unfortunately, the businessman [Bristow] did not own a heli-copter. [To solve this problem, he planned] … to obtain an S-61 aircraft under lease to Okanagan from Sikorsky. When Okanagan refused to release the machine, the deal was stymied. As a solu-tion, Okanagan bought out Bristow, launched a subsidiary, called Universal Helicopters, and transferred the S-61 lease to Universal."

"I learned a long time ago that you can't dance with every-body," Harry Steele comments today. "And I had a history with Okanagan. When Bristow called, I told them I wasn't interested in a partnership."

Before all of this occurred, however, Bristow and Steele met in Steele's Albatross Hotel in Gander. "Bristow was pretty flashy," Harry says. "He arrived with a pouch full of expensive cigars and did a lot of big talking. I told him again that my association with Okanagan ruled out any partnership. Then I said, 'There's a guy down in St. John's who owns a helicopter company, maybe you should go and talk to him, and he did.'" And so, Bristow con-tacted Craig Dobbin.

On his way to Britain to negotiate with Bristow, Dobbin flew out of Gander, staying overnight at Harry Steele's Gander hotel and popping in the next morning at Harry's office for a quick farewell. Craig was in a rush to do a big business deal, and he had to touch base with a financier to cement the funding for the deal, but he made sure that he had time to see Harry.

Business initially brought them together, but it was Harry and Craig's mutual love of salmon fishing that cemented their personal connection. "It was a joke. Every June they would go off fishing, just the two of them, and Craig always said that it was too early to be going up to Labrador and Craig told him it would be snowing and raining upside down. Harry convinced him to go, and they'd usually venture out around June 6th," says Elaine Dobbin.

———————

As a successful local businessman, Craig Dobbin took up what is in many ways a rich man's pastime: salmon fishing. It takes money to get to the good rivers. Salmon rivers in Labrador are remote and the best way to get to them is by helicopter. Craig looked into buying a helicopter and realized the only way he could afford it — he was successful but he was not that rich yet — was to own it and lease it out. That is just what he did.

"Craig loved to salmon fish and he hated relying on anyone else to have to go and he wanted to get to the best salmon rivers and the only way to do that was by helicopter and he did get a helicopter but he realized that it was a very expensive toy and one that he couldn't afford," says Elaine. "So he started leasing it when he wasn't using it and found a niche and an opportunity. Hence Sealand was born and that became Canadian Helicopter Corporation, which was the largest helicopter company in the world outside of the U.S. and Russian military."

Sealand Helicopters was founded in February of 1977. At first, it ran charters; some were flights to salmon rivers, but there were also runs to mining and construction sites on the island of Newfoundland and mainland Labrador.

Then, in 1979, came an event that changed the economy of Newfoundland and Craig Dobbin's future: the discovery of the Hibernia oil field off the southeast coast of Labrador. There were two ways to get there: by ship and by helicopter. Sealand Helicopter and Craig Dobbin seized the opportunity. He was in the perfect spot; he owned a Newfoundland company ready and able to ferry workers to the offshore rigs. Servicing the oil business not only generated a lot of money, it also allowed the company to build up expertise that could be used anywhere in the world. Sealand Helicopters expanded, operating all over the world. In 1987 it merged with two other firms, including Okanagan Helicopters, to form CHC Helicopter.

Barry Clouter has a connection to both men. He worked for Harry at Eastern Provincial Airways, and the companies that swallowed it, for about thirty years, and when he retired from the airline business in 2000 he went to work for Craig at CHC Helicopter in Halifax.

Harry was on the board of CHC and knew Barry Clouter could handle whatever Craig threw at him. And he certainly threw him in the deep end. "I managed [the] North and South America business units. I travelled out of Halifax to all the places nobody else wanted to go, like Ecuador, Venezuela, and Surinam. I had about ten years at CHC," says Barry. "We were an offshore transportation provider — passengers and freight. There would have been a fair amount of business back in those days so requests would come out and we would bid on the business. In Venezuela, we had two bases if you can believe it. It was my responsibility was to manage the operations there, their profitability and whatever else. It's an exciting business."

Barry Clouter is still agog at the size of the firm Craig created. "When you think about where it started: the guy had one or two machines and grew it into the largest offshore helicopter company in the world. We had over three hundred and fifty helicopters. Back then, Craig was the first to put the Super Puma in Newfoundland. And in later years we got into Sikorsky S-92s and Eurocopters, but in the end, it was mostly eighteen to twenty-passenger helicopters, Sikorsky S-61 we called them, it was the commercial version of the military Sea King, carrying people and gear back and forth to the oil rigs."

Running a helicopter company was, and presumably still is, an incredibly lucrative business. Craig Dobbin took risks, but he also reaped the rewards. Just one helicopter could be a money earner, but put together a fleet of 350 of them, and you create a money machine. "To this day, I still can't believe how much revenue a small helicopter can generate. To give you an example, you could have one helicopter and generate a million dollars a month," says Barry.

Craig turned CHC into a hugely successful company, but he relied on Harry, who was on the board, to help guide him. This happened perhaps not despite but because of their differences. Clouter remembers, "Harry would say to me, 'Craig used to ask me for advice, and I'd gladly give it knowing it was not going anywhere.'"

A good line, but not really true. One example involves a situation that arose concerning the board of directors of CHC.

In October of 2005, CHC was listed on the New York Stock Exchange. Ever the showman, Craig had an EC 225 Twinstar helicopter flown to New York City and parked in front of the Stock Exchange on the morning of the listing.

The listing came with new strict reporting requirements, and that is where Harry advised his friend. The American securities rule known as the Sarbanes-Oxley Act would require Craig to clean up his board. Having sound businessmen like Harry Steele and financier Steve Hudson on the board was one thing, but including salmon fishing pals and the former Canadian ambassador to Ireland — Craig was a sentimental Irishman — was another.

Harry was on the board of CHC Helicopters, and Craig was on the board of NCC. On one occasion Craig was thinking about dropping some members of the CHC board. Harry thought it was a rash idea and talked him out of it. In the mid-1980s Craig wanted to buy a British-based helicopter company. It would have been a massive investment, and Craig was keen on it, but Harry was not.

"Craig tried everything to buy it, and Harry talked Craig out of it saying it would have destroyed him," recalls Elaine Dobbin. "Craig did give up on it afterwards strictly on Harry's advice. Craig didn't like to walk away from a deal, but he did in this case."

In the end, of course, deals are likely to be forgotten but friendships remain. Over many years, in all sorts of circumstances — around boardroom tables and in their favourite fishing camps —

Harry and Craig maintained their close friendship. Toward the end of his life, Craig went to Florida to visit Harry. It was one of their last meetings. John Lawrence Reynolds describes it in his book on Dobbin:

> Visiting Florida that summer, Craig invited Harry Steele to the Clearwater Airport to show off his new private helicopter. Steele noted the craft had skids, not wheels, meaning it couldn't land at Long Harbour or Adlatok, and Dobbin explained that he would build landing pads at all of his locations so he could land anywhere in the new machine. Steele wondered about that. Not about building the pads but about Dobbin's claim that he would continue to fly back and forth to the fishing camps. Dobbin wore Gucci slippers not shoes that day because his feet were so swollen.
>
> Steele believed his friend's end was near and so, it appears, did Craig Dobbin. It was Steele to whom Craig turned a few weeks later when reviewing his will, mentioning friends, associates, and CHC employees he wanted to recognize after his death. "Did I leave anyone out?" he would ask and whenever Steele would mention someone Craig would add his or her name. Finally, Harry begged off, fearing his friend's generosity could dilute his estate severely. There were more than sixty people named in Craig Dobbin's will. He left his friend Harry Steele his beloved Adlatok fishing camp in Labrador.

Seymour Schulich saw the closeness between the two men. "When Craig died, something went out of Harry's life," says Seymour.

NCC published a tribute on the death of Craig Dobbin: "Newfoundland Capital Corporation notes with sadness and affection the passing of Craig Laurence Dobbin, a member of our Board (April 15, 1994, to October 7, 2006), the head and founder of CHC Helicopter Corporation, entrepreneur, outdoorsman, and to many of this Company both an inspiration and a deep friend."

Harry gave one of the eulogies at his friend's funeral. Dobbin's biographer described it as "more poignant" than the others:

> Craig Dobbin was singular in the scope of his accomplishments and the reach of his personality. He brought to his business career a combination of adventure, inventiveness, and daring. The path he followed was one uniquely carved by himself. His record achievements flowed from an intelligence and character equally unique.
>
> In business, he was a perfect illustration of the sometimes loosely-applied description: a self-made man. He began, as he put it himself, during the Convocation at Memorial University awarding him the honorary degree of Doctor of Laws, "literally, at the bottom." The reference was to his early years as a commercial diver who "worked" the waters of St. John's Harbour.
>
> Beginning in the early sixties in real estate, and branching from there by a plan known only to himself, he eventually became the CEO and owner of the world's largest helicopter firm. It is worth noting that with CHC Helicopter Corporation, Craig Dobbin established another milestone: of being the first Newfoundland businessman of whom it may be said that he established, from Newfoundland, a genuine, fully international company.
>
> Within the business community of Atlantic Canada it is not necessary to detail the scope and quality of his business career, merely to make the pointed note

that even within a community known for strong leadership and entrepreneurial flair, Craig Dobbin was a standout performer and a standout success.

His personality could not be confined even by the intense demands of starting, developing, expanding, and maintaining his business interests. His hobbies and pastimes would claim the energy of an ordinary man. His passion for the outdoors, his love of flying and fishing, gave him a name (and friends) that spanned the continent.

His fishing camps at Long Harbour in Newfoundland and on the great Labrador salmon rivers were often gatherings of business people, politicians, writers, friends, and fellow sportsmen. Craig Dobbin had high enthusiasms, and he found as much passion in sharing what he loved as in the enthusiasms themselves. He was an open and generous friend, and a great (and frequently silent) supporter of people in hard moments of their lives, be they friends or not.

Perhaps the overriding character of this exceptional man was his unquenchable love for Newfoundland itself. He was a Newfoundlander in everything he did, most of what he said, and in many of those things he held closest and dearest. Canada was his beloved country, the passion for Newfoundland the fire within the core.

Those that called him friend, among whom the many shareholders and employees of Newfoundland Capital Corporation, miss him greatly, wish him remembered, and in words that are frequently applied but rarely as just as they are in his case, note "that we shall not see his like again."

Craig Dobbin was here, big time!

Fifteen

Universal Helicopters

It all depended on the economy and who wanted to mine. Hype about mining and exploration. Forest fires were excellent.
— Kay Williams on the helicopter business

Universal Helicopters was one of the few companies Harry owned outside the umbrella of Newfoundland Capital Corporation, and one of the companies he took a personal interest in; among other things, its choppers flew him and his guests to fishing camps. It was more than that, though. He liked the down to earth people who ran it: Paul Williams and his wife, Kay, and Norm Noseworthy — all Newfoundlanders.

Newfoundland swarmed with helicopters in the early 1980s. The development of the Hibernia oil field and offshore drilling created a need for helicopters, since they offered the only means to fly to the rigs. As well, there was a great deal of other development going on at the time: the preliminary work on the Gull Island hydroelectric project and Inco's mining development at Voisey's Bay.

Okanagan Helicopters of British Columbia ran everything at first. It owned Universal Helicopters, which had operated in Newfoundland and Labrador since the early 1960s. Harry Steele was asked to go on the board of directors of Okanagan.

Paul Williams of Universal Helicopters with the arctic char.

At the time, Okanagan offered services across Canada, and had some international operations as well. In the end, the company was stretched too thin and it went under. Craig Dobbin took over the company. After a short time, it was re-named CHC, and went on to become an international success.

Separate from that, Harry, the late Paul Williams, and Norm Noseworthy acquired Universal Helicopters, with Harry owning the controlling shareholding.

Long before that happened, however, Paul Williams was the base manager for Universal Helicopters at Goose Bay, Labrador. When he arrived, there were only two or three helicopters on site, but it eventually grew to as many as twenty. The workhorse of the fleet was the Bell 206 Jet Ranger, a versatile helicopter manufactured in Canada.

"When Harry went on the board, and the offshore oil started going really good, my husband was asked to go to St. John's," says Kay Williams, Paul's widow.* "We both moved to St. John's, and from there it just evolved into Universal breaking away and Harry buying the shares from Okanagan when they went bankrupt."

Harry Steele and Paul Williams took over Universal Helicopters in 1987. It became Universal Helicopters Newfoundland, and it restricted its operation to Newfoundland and Labrador. It flew only VFR, or visual flight rules. They immediately got out of the offshore helicopter business, which operated under IFR, or instrument flight rules. To the outsider, it may have seemed a potential goldmine, but Kay Williams says the opposite was true.

"It wasn't a gold mine. It could [have been], I suppose, but it was a hard place to make money, and the offshore was starting to wind down, and a lot of the companies weren't drilling anymore. It wasn't the place to be at that time."

Universal Helicopters main base of operations was Goose Bay,** but it also had four other smaller bases: Gander, St. John's,

---

* Kay Williams worked with her husband at Universal for many years, staying on even after he died young of cancer at the age of fifty-four. She remembers she loved living in Goose Bay. Life there was simple and uncomplicated.

"People would find this surprising, but the weather in Goose Bay is pretty good. I had a small child, so it wasn't the big hassle of him having to go here or there to go to school, and it was just easier. Life was good," remembers Kay.

** Universal Helicopters was right on the base at Goose Bay. At the time it was used by NATO air forces for low-level training over the Russian-like terrain of remote Labrador. Italian pilots would fly twenty feet above the runway, upside down.

Pasadena near Corner Brook, and one in Mill-Town Bay d'Espoir on the south coast of Newfoundland.

"There was one helicopter based here in Gander, one in Mill-Town Bay d'Espoir, two in Pasadena, and probably ten or eleven based out of Goose Bay, but they all went around to all the bases. There might be eight in Goose Bay, and they might have a lot of work down here, and they'd ferry the work down here," says Kay.

Most of the helicopters were Jet Rangers, but there was a gradual shift to Bell Long Rangers, which could stay in the air for two and a half to three hours, against two hours for the Jet Rangers. It is 831 kilometres from Goose Bay to St. John's as the helicopter flies and the Long Ranger can do it non-stop if there isn't too much of a headwind.

"When the company was bought in 1987, I was vice-president of maintenance, and a year or so later I became executive vice-president of the company, and I remained there as executive VP of the company and director of maintenance until the company was sold," remembers Norm Noseworthy, who with the Williams was a minority shareholder. "We started with nine helicopters, and I think we got as high as twenty-two, but I'm not quite sure. But we generally operated twenty or twenty-one helicopters. They were owned, but we used to lease one or a couple now and then for specific jobs.

"Newfoundland and Labrador cover 405,212 square kilometres, an area just a little bit smaller than Sweden. To do forestry work on the island[,] … rescue people from remote native communities, or survey bear and caribou populations, [you need a helicopter, and so that] meant there was a lot of work for government departments such as forestry, health and wildlife. The federal government was also a client since it seems it can never make up its mind on buying its own helicopters.

"Harry is a dealmaker rather than a hands-on [operator], but he took a keen interest in Universal, perhaps more so than any other firm he owned, except Eastern Provincial Airlines.

"He was continually hands-on but not involved in the day-to-day. I would talk to him every week for sure and sometimes two or three times a week. He wanted to know what was happening and what was going on and [wanted] to know what I was doing. One of my responsibilities was the buying and selling of aircraft, so he was very interested in that and what I was doing and where I was going and how I was making deals and that sort of thing," says Noseworthy.

"I would consider it … a profitable business, and I think he would as well. The helicopter business is seasonal, and we were in a bit of a cyclical downturn when he bought the company, and it was only a year or so after that when it started to come up during the forest fires, for which they need a lot of helicopters of course. Then Voisey's Bay was discovered, and helicopters and mining became very active, which it hadn't been for quite some time. [At the time, the Long Ranger was running about a thousand dollars an hour plus fuel and pilot expenses.] That was a big boost for the company in its early stages."

The busiest season for Universal Helicopters was from June to the end of September or October, depending on the weather. Forest fires meant extra flying time. More critical than the weather was the economy. If there was a mining rush, the helicopters were flying non-stop. One of those periods was the opening up of Voisey's Bay. It was a giant discovery, and it seemed every prospector in Canada wanted to fly in and stake a claim.

The Voisey's Bay rush ran from 1994 to 1997. "There were some real characters, prospectors and people from junior mining companies, who came in from Toronto, Vancouver, and Montreal. The helicopters were busy, but so were the bars and restaurants in Goose Bay and St. John's.

"The Voisey's Bay discovery brought in all the junior mining companies, and of course everybody wants to make the big find, so there were a lot of people in the area. They prospected and drilled all over the place. We were carrying the prospecting teams, and bringing back things like core samples from their drilling," says Kay Williams.

Almost all of that exploration flying had to be done in the late spring to early fall. Summer was the time of the year when Harry and his guests would go fishing in Labrador, so helicopters were needed to take them north. It was also the time when Harry would come over to talk business with Paul and Kay Williams on his way to and from his fishing camps.

"Working with Harry was perfect. I wouldn't say it if it weren't, believe me, but it was absolutely great," says Kay, who is a straight shooter and says what she means. "He was a decisive man. There's no problem for anybody to work with Harry as long as you do your work."

It wasn't all quiet on the Universal front, however. Harry would argue with Kay and Paul over things, issues such as whether they should build a new hangar at Goose Bay. They wanted it; Harry didn't. The big hangar did get built.

"Paul did win the argument, [and] after the new hangar was built, the place was such an improvement that HRS was quite pleased with the outcome," says Kay.

Norm Noseworthy agrees that working with Harry was good, though he does say the relationship "had its ups and downs. Harry was a great guy to work for. He was very fair but when he wanted a job done he wanted it done. I found him very good to work with and to deal with as a partner and as a friend," says Noseworthy.

Harry sold Universal Helicopters in September of 2014, and the buyer came through his connection to Paul Martin, the former prime minister of Canada. After Martin left politics in 2006, he and Harry saw more of each other. As a politician and as a private citizen, Martin had a keen interest in helping Indigenous communities. He set up a charitable operation called CAPE, Capital for Aboriginal Prosperity and Entrepreneurship.

"I put in two or three million (dollars) of my own, and I raised it from a bunch of banks. It was a fifty-million-dollar fund to invest in Indigenous entrepreneurship. The Inuit wanted to buy Harry's helicopter company and run it as an Inuit-owned enterprise," says Martin.

"The Inuit approached CAPE, saying they wanted to buy this helicopter company from Harry Steele. Harry had told me that he was going to sell it and so I put the two of them together. CAPE ended up being one of the major shareholders in buying this, along with the Inuit."

Universal Helicopters still operates today, owned by Indigenous groups, a partnership of companies formed by Nunatsiavut Group of Companies, Tasiujatsoak Trust, and CAPE Fund.

Sixteen

Catherine Thornhill Steele

There's a lot about business, my son, that's not very nice.

— Words of wisdom from
Catherine Steele to her boys

Catherine Steele is as responsible for Harry's success as he is. First, the two of them share a lifelong love affair; each supports the other unconditionally.

"My mother and father were a team, I know that's a cliché with a lot of people, but with them, it's very true. Besides being husband and wife, from the business point of view, they had very complementary but different skill sets," says Peter Steele.

Catherine is frugal, ambitious in her own way, and loves business. Her early forays into real estate, along with Harry's success in the stock market, paved the way for their joint business success. Though she was raising her three boys, Peter, John, and Rob, Catherine came up with the idea of buying distressed residential properties in Dartmouth.

"I was looking for houses that were in bankruptcy so I could buy them, fix them up, and hopefully make some money," says Catherine. "I studied music at the university, but I found that I had an affinity for business and I enjoyed it."

She bought and renovated three houses in Dartmouth that were in foreclosure. When Harry was posted to Gander, she

The Albatross Hotel, Gander, Newfoundland.

started to look for similar opportunities. But Gander was a much smaller place, with a lot of government-owned housing connected to the airbase. There was not a large pool of housing to choose from, never mind trying to find a property in foreclosure.

The bank Catherine dealt with did have one interesting property, but it was a hotel, not a house: The Albatross, a rather apt name given the disastrous financial state it was in.

Catherine Steele transformed The Albatross from a hotel with forty-eight rooms, one cook, and two waitresses, into one with one hundred and thirteen rooms, five cooks, and twelve waitresses. The success of The Albatross Hotel was the foundation of Harry Steele's business career. He could not have done it without his wife.

Catherine remembers those early days: "When I was in Dartmouth, I bought a few houses that were in bankruptcy, and I fixed them up and sold them, so I went to the bank to see if there were any such things here in Gander. They said no, but we do have a hotel here that's in bankruptcy and would I be interested. That's how it all started. So I went to the bank, and they lent us the money. I don't think it had been run very well at all," says Catherine, too polite to be overly critical of the former owners, even five decades on. She set about to teach herself how to run a hotel and went about it in a logical way.

"The Albatross wasn't a fascinating place, but as soon as I got it I went to the library in Gander, and I found a book entitled *Every Customer Is My Guest*. I read that, and I met with the staff, and I would discuss things with them and what they felt would make their jobs a lot better. I will never forget one of the girls said to me, 'Mrs. Steele, could we possibly have a pocket in our uniform to keep our tips in?' I hadn't thought of that, but I remember that to this day."

Every Customer Is My Guest is 112-page book put out by the Department of Tourism of Nova Scotia in 1964 and reprinted several times. Its object is to help the owners of small hotels and restaurants. The book gives advice on the food side of the business, pointing out that waste costs money. *Every Customer Is My Guest* may have been written fifty-five years ago, but its advice is quite modern.

It talks about self-respect, both for the employee and the employer, and advises on how to handle difficult customers. Example: "The overfamiliar guest: Be courteous, dignified, and ladylike. Avoid long conversations. Stay away from the table except when actual service is needed. Never try to give a 'wise-crack' answer to a 'smart' remark. You will only cheapen yourself and lower yourself to the rudeness of the guest."

Added to the book's advice was Catherine's common sense.

"I knew how I would like to be treated and I felt that I wanted people to feel as if they had come to my house. They don't leave saying, 'Well, I've been there twice, the first and the last time'; that they would enjoy their visit and want to come back. That was precisely the way I wanted people to feel about this business. Once this lady came to me and said that the waitress had asked us if we enjoyed our meal and that has stuck with me to this day.

"I was very happy about that because I loved business. I like people. I loved the hotel business and working with the staff because I was learning as they were learning."

Under Catherine Steele's management, The Albatross Hotel was an immediate success. While Catherine ran the hotel, Harry would drum up business by speaking to airline crews landing at Gander.

"Mum ran the hotel, organizing the menus and all that stuff, while Dad was busy in the navy but trying to drum up some business for the hotel," says Rob Steele, sitting in the dining room at The Albatross. "Eastern Provincial Airways was based here in Gander at the time, and the Crosbie family owned it, and the flight crews would all stay at a competing hotel. So, my father called on the airline to try to get them to re-direct that business to his hotel. That's how he struck up an acquaintance with Keith Miller, who was then president of EPA."

That was the foundation of the success of the hotel, which the family owns to this day.

International flights also helped, as word spread about The Albatross being a decent place to stay. Gander was a refueling stop on the way to Europe; planes going to Cuba couldn't fly over U.S. airspace, so they, too, had to stop, coming and going.

At one stage, rooms at The Albatross were in such demand that the same room could be meticulously cleaned and rented out again on the same day after flight crews had taken a short kip before resuming their journey, whether it was east, west, or south. All flightpaths led to Gander.

The Steeles later acquired another hotel, the Sinbad. Catherine explains that the two are quite different. "If it's a special event, you would go to Sinbad's, whereas The Albatross is more for travellers. But it was all new to me. My dad was a fisherman, so business wasn't on my radar at all," says Catherine. "Both hotels benefited from being in the same town as one of the busiest airports in the world. Being in Gander, the airport was the vital part of the town, and we got just about all of them. We had all the pilots and flight crews staying at the hotel."

Janet Catherine Thornhill was born in Grand Bank, Newfoundland, into a prominent local family. The village of Grand Bank is on the southern tip of the Burin Peninsula. It is one of the warmest spots in all of Newfoundland, and its harbour is ice-free year round, one of the reasons it was the centre of the fishery.

It is a small place with a lot of history. Grand Bank is only forty-eight kilometres from St. Pierre, which, with its sister island of Miquelon, is the sole territory of France left in North America. Catherine's hometown was once known as Grand Banc and was owned by France. It was ceded to England after a European war that France lost. As negotiated in the Treaty of Paris in 1763, England ceded St. Pierre and Miquelon back to France. The English inhabitants of those islands moved to Grand Bank, spelt with an English *k*, not a French *c*.

Catherine came from an accomplished family. Her mother, Ruth Williams, was a schoolteacher, an educated woman with a university degree from a college in the American state of Kentucky. Her father was a sea captain, a profession held in great respect in Newfoundland. They were a solid middle-class family, with a way of life far from the subsistence living of Musgrave Harbour. Despite the comfort of her upbringing, Catherine always felt it was important to work hard and succeed. She felt her father lived a precarious existence, even if he was successful and held in high esteem.

By the time that Catherine was born, her father, Captain Arch Thornhill, was a legendary deep-sea fishing captain. He had started around 1918, fishing offshore in a dory, often with his brother or his cousin. Arch Thornhill recalled in the early 1920s he made only three hundred dollars one year. But he was determined to make good.

"I never gave up once in my life," he said. He said that as a young man he fished in a dory for seventy-two hours straight without sleep. That determination passed down to his children: Catherine, who was pivotal in Harry Steele's success, and her brother, Roland Thornhill, a successful stockbroker and a man who was once deputy premier of the province of Nova Scotia.

The rich fishing grounds of the Grand Banks are off the southern coast of Newfoundland, where the frigid Labrador Current, travelling down the coast of Labrador from the Arctic, meets the warm waters of the Gulfstream. Cold meeting warm means the sea is often shrouded in fog.

Arch Thornhill's first command as a skipper was a schooner owned out of Nova Scotia. He borrowed one hundred dollars from a friend to buy two shares in the *Vera P. Thornhill*. It was February of 1927, and he was twenty-seven years old. His first trip he commanded twenty-four men in the 170-ton, eleven-dory vessel. The dories would leave the mother ship, go out and fish, and return to the main vessel.

The schooner was all sail, no engine, at the mercy of the sea and the wind. On the first voyage, the wind pushed them into Gulf of St. Lawrence ice. It would be a while before the schooner he worked was fitted with an auxiliary engine.

The first trip was a success, and Captain Thornhill returned with "almost six hundred quintals of fish."* There were even bigger catches, but the crew's luck eventually ran out, the majority owners of the vessel balked, and Captain Thornhill, one of the youngest skippers in Newfoundland, had to wait for his next ship. He went on to other schooners, including the *Ronald George*, which sailed in dangerous waters during the war.

Eventually, he went on to big trawlers, including the *Blue Foam* and the *Blue Spray*. On his thirty-eight trips on the *Blue*

---

* A quintal equals 112 pounds (51 kilograms). So that trip brought in about thirty thousand kilograms of fish.

The Thornhill family. Back (l-r): Captain Archibald Thornhill and Roland; Front (l-r): Cyril, Mrs. Ruth (Williams) Thornhill, Florence, and Catherine.

The Thornhill family in Grand Bank (l-r): Florence, Roland, Cyril, and Catherine.

"The Vera P. Thornhill"
In Lunenburg Harbour
The very first vessel that Arch commanded and was he ever proud of her

Vera Thornhill, Arch Thornhill's schooner.

Foam, he landed 2.7 million kilograms of haddock, cod, and other fish; just twenty-eight trips on the *Blue Spray* landed 2.4 million kilograms.

"Arch Thornhill was a very quiet and very modest individual. A very intelligent guy," says Raoul Andersen, the professor from Memorial University who wrote a biography of Arch Thornhill, *Voyage to the Grand Banks: The Saga of Captain Arch Thornhill*. "He was not a big man, but he was not a man who was afraid to tell people that he had employed as members of the crew to meet their obligation to do work. He didn't hesitate to tell a man that he had to get his rear end in gear or that kind of thing."

Later in life, Arch became close with Peter Steele, his eldest grandson on the Steele side. "My grandfather Thornhill was my mentor. He and I were particularly close, and he was an interesting man. The context of Newfoundland society at the time was five or six families in St. John's controlled the economy under the banner of the Water Street merchants," says Peter.

"One of the assets or the pillars of the Newfoundland economy that they controlled was obviously the fishing industry, as well as the import of whatever and the export of fish. People needed staples and consumer goods and so on. My grandfather was one of a very small group of [middle-class] people in Newfoundland society. He wasn't in the Water Street merchants, but he worked himself up from rowing in the dory to being the captain of first, ships under sail, large commercial vessels, and then on as a captain when they became motorized. I knew both my grandparents very well.

"My grandmother's name was Ruth Williams. The Williamses are a very storied and accomplished family in Newfoundland. My grandmother was a teacher in one of those one- and two-room schoolhouses in a different part of Newfoundland than Musgrave Harbour, up around the Pool's Cove area where the Williamses were from. She obtained her education degree from, of all places, a university in Kentucky."

Almost all Arch Thornhill's fishing was on the Grand Banks. The weather could be violent, and he knew many men who met their death at sea. He told Peter the story of a giant wave washing everything off the deck of a schooner. Although no one perished, one man had to dive down a hatch to save himself. On another occasion, the cannon misfired when he was setting it off to tell the dories to come back to the mother ship. It blinded him temporarily, but he recovered.

It wasn't all fishing. There was a voyage to Barbados, to bring cargo and pick up rum. The major problem there was he was not experienced in sailing in warm waters. Not a major concern. Many seafaring men split their time between working cargo and fishing. When they would sail their schooners far afield, "many 'went foreign' as work required," writes Raoul Andersen.

Arch Thornhill's trip to Barbados was in the winter of 1931. He carried a cargo of lumber on the way down and rum and molasses on the voyage home. The owner of the schooner paid him an extra five dollars for a job well done.

"I swore I would never marry anyone who went to sea because my dad went to sea and I saw how my mum worried," says Catherine. She remembers a time when her father was gone for seven days, and no one knew if he was alive or dead. He was sailing from the Grand Banks to Burin on the south coast of Newfoundland.

"A big storm came up, and he had to put the vessel out to sea and in those days on those ships they had no communication whatsoever. My mother had four children. I was the oldest, and I knew she was trying to keep up her spirits but I knew how worried she was and I promised myself then that I would never … and you should never say never … I would never marry anybody who went to sea. And look at this," says Catherine in a joking way, an obvious reference to Harry's years in the navy. "But I thought when I first met him that maybe I would meet somebody else through him. But he's very convincing and look at me here sixty-three years later."

Harry, of course, has lived long and prospered since his days in the navy, and Catherine's father, too, survived his life on the seas. Captain Thornhill retired from fishing in 1962 and died in 1977, one of the last schooner captains of the Grand Banks.

Catherine studied music at Mount Allison University, quite an achievement for a girl from Grand Bank, if only because getting there in the 1940s was not easy. Grand Bank, not to be confused with the fishing grounds known as the Grand Banks, is a town on the southern tip of the Burin Peninsula. Catherine explains the route she took, first heading north to get to the destination far south of her hometown.

"When I went to Mount A I was living in Grand Bank, so I got a taxi to take me to the centre of the island, and from there I got the train to Port-aux-Basques, where I got the boat over to Sydney. In Sydney I got a train to take me to Mount Allison. That was how I got to university. I don't remember now, but days it seemed endless. Travel was terrible, but it was worth it."

That might seem an exaggeration to the modern ear, but the train that crossed Newfoundland was slow. The train, on its narrow gauge tracks, took twenty-three hours to travel from St. John's to Port-aux-Basques and the ferry terminal there. The ferry to Sydney was another fourteen hours, and then there was a train to Mount Allison. It took determination to get there.

Catherine met Harry when she came back to Newfoundland with her music degree and started to teach. The couple met at a church dance, a chaperoned affair designed to allow young people to get to know each other.

"I started dating him when he was going to Memorial University, and I was teaching at Prince of Wales," recalls Catherine. She remembers she loved teaching even though not all of her students were born to music.

"Some parents wanted their children to take music, and they didn't have a musical bone in their body, but you did your best with what you had. I loved teaching, and I loved the children, and in the summer I would drive around town to see if any of them were outside playing or anything so that I could have a chat with them."

Their firstborn son, Peter, knows the family history, including things that happened before he was born, such as his parent's courtship. "My father was in St. John's studying education at Memorial, and my mother was living in St. John's and they met there," says Peter. "Back then a lot of people met and entered into courtship or were introduced to each other before courtship through church-sponsored dances and activities that were chaperoned and supervised. They met through the United Church–sponsored activity and from that introduction things evolved until they got married." Catherine was twenty-four when they married on Harry's twenty-fifth birthday.

Catherine left teaching soon after their marriage because Harry was transferred to England. She loved living there.

Catherine Thornhill at her graduating piano recital, Mount Allison University.

People who got to know Harry Steele later in his business career came to admire Catherine as much as they did Harry.

"She's a terrific lady, very kind. Her father was the last of the captains of the schooners," says David Bruce, who was born in Scotland and was one of Harry's prime stockbrokers in Toronto. "They had a hard upbringing, as they all did on Newfoundland. She wouldn't see her father for months at a time when he went over to the Grand Banks. She knew the day he was leaving because he used to leave a silver coin underneath her egg cup. She always looked underneath the egg cup for the coin, and she'd know he was leaving for a voyage.

"She is very musically minded, and her father bought her a piano when she was eight or nine years old. They brought it onto the deck of the schooner, and they lifted it off the boat up to the house, and she has been playing the piano ever since."

Seymour Schulich, the mining entrepreneur and philanthropist, donated a chair of music in Catherine's honour at McGill University.

Rex Murphy, perhaps the most famous son of Newfoundland because of his broadcasting on the CBC and his opinion columns in the *National Post*, remembers The Albatross and how hard Catherine worked to make it a success. Rex would visit the hotel when he was filing items for CBC television.

"I remember we would go on our shoots and it was a thing we'd go to The Albatross because the food was so good. And that was all the small kitchen and Mrs. Steele making sure that they put out good grub. I stress this that it's very true that [out of] the family and Schulich and Craig Dobbin, Catherine is the key. That union is a union, and even with all his bluster, Catherine still has equal standing. He's a great patriarch, but, in fact, there are two people fused into one. You're not taking on just him; you're taking on both of them."

Seventeen

Fishing Tales

I never see a Labrador Discount on these legal bills.

— Harry Steele on his
lawyers fishing in Labrador

As a boy, Harry Steele fished for cod and other fish with his father just off the coast from Musgrave Harbour. Later in life, when he could afford it, he went fishing for salmon in Labrador. He could land a dry fly with the best of them, trying to tease the salmon into biting.

But his wife, Catherine, says it wasn't salmon he was after. "As one of our boys said, 'Dad doesn't go fishing for fish; he goes fishing for business.'"

Harry owns five fishing camps, two in Newfoundland and three in Labrador. His favourite is on the Adlatok River on the north coast of Labrador near a community called Hopedale, an hour and twenty minutes north of Goose Bay by helicopter, and just south of Voisey's Bay. There is another way to get there: fly to Hopedale and take an hour-long trip in a speedboat. The camp is right on salt water. The camp is one he co-owned with the late Frank Moores, the former premier of Newfoundland and successful lobbyist, who would spend entire summers at his fishing lodge. Harry would go up for shorter periods, entertaining such

Adlatok from the air.

diverse people as the president of the United States and the late author and bon vivant Mordecai Richler.

Most fishing camps charge their customers a fair piece of change for a five-day week. For the most part, the Steele fishing camps have guests up for two or three days; the difference is they don't charge the guests.

"It's all corporate networking, but it's not something where you're going to generate a bottom line. We don't charge anything. It's totally *gratis*; we absorb the entire cost," says Rob Steele.

Craig Dobbin told a reporter for the *National Post* in 1996: "He [Harry] does on the fishing stream what others do on the golf course."

There are a lot of top business types in Canada who want to fish in Labrador. Because a place like Adlatok is so isolated, it doesn't get fished out. Atlantic salmon swim up the river to spawn. They aren't hungry, so you have to annoy them to get them to bite at a fly. It takes skill and patience, but a fighting salmon on a fly line is a thrill many people desire.

Harry was well respected as a corporate director and a self-made man, but people he didn't even know were lining up to

President George H.W. Bush's catch (l-r): Harry Steele, Johnny Morris, Ken Raynor, Howard Wolf, George H.W. Bush, Elaine Dobbin, Jean Charest, John Crosbie, and Craig Dobbin.

Fishing buddies: George H.W. Bush and Harry R. Steele.

spend time at his camps in Labrador. The most illustrious guest was the late George H.W. Bush, former president of the United States, vice-president under Ronald Reagan, and one-time director of the CIA.

Harry recalls: "He let it be known through somebody who worked for him that he wanted to fish in Labrador. I said 'Do you realize the work involved in getting him up to Labrador? How the heck are you ever going to do it or can it even be done?' I tried to put it together, and it took so many people because of the security in bringing the former president of the United States up there. The funny thing about it was that Craig Dobbin went down to Kennebunkport (President Bush's summer home) to look around. Craig came back up and spent a fortune on the camp to get it ready for the president. The sad thing was that Craig got sick and couldn't come up anymore, so I had to try to piece the stuff together. So, I got him up there, and a native fellow told me about a great fishing place over on the Adlatok River."

Harry remembers getting up early one morning and there was some rustling in the kitchen. Sure enough, it was George H.W. Bush making coffee at 5:00 a.m. That far north, the sun was already up. The two men started talking. The former president, a navy man, was interested in Harry's career. Then Harry asked him what was the most important job he'd done.

"I figured he'd say president of the United States, but he said head of the CIA," recalls Harry. There is no record about whether the two men talked about spycraft, something each of them knew well. Harry did say of him: "He's a nice man, without working at it. Fantastic man. I went up with him three times. He's the best."

President Bush did not travel alone. Before the presidential group arrived, an advance party flew up to Labrador to check the camp out. There was a significant Secret Service detail with him, five of them, and one RCMP officer. This caused much joking about the one Mountie doing the work of five Secret Service men.

"The thing they did was take our bear gun, the gun we used for nuisance bears. That was all done days before Mr. Bush came up," says Greg Baikie, the helicopter pilot who also looks after the camp.

Harry bonded with the president, his kind of guy and a former U.S. Navy pilot, as did Craig Dobbin. On one trip, in July of 1993, just six months after he left office, George H.W. Bush witnessed a sales agreement between Craig Dobbin and Harry Steele transferring ownership of the fishing lodge on the Adlatok River from Dobbin to Steele.

Long before a former president of the United States went fishing with Harry, a future prime minister of Canada was up there. Paul Martin met Harry and his pal Craig Dobbin in the early 1980s before Paul entered politics. At the time, he was the main shareholder of Canada Steamship Lines, a business that was related to some of the holdings of Newfoundland Capital Corporation.

"I really took to Harry. His story was so wonderful: a former naval officer who goes into business. He was larger than life. From then on we had a friendship much more than a business relationship," says the former Liberal prime minister.

The friendship went both ways. "Not only is he a good businessman, but he's also a straight shooter," says Harry. Paul Martin may be the only Liberal politician Harry ever supported. The two men never did business; they were just friends.

"I also got to know Craig Dobbin," says Paul. "He and Harry used to go salmon fishing every year, and I used to be a salmon fisherman, and they invited me to go fishing with them. I probably went fishing with Harry and Craig Dobbin two or three times. Craig had a camp which I think was on the Hunt River.

"My experience going fishing with Harry and Craig was that I don't ever remember seeing either one of them put a rod in the water and I had been fishing with them, as I said, two or three times. I used to love salmon fishing and one day when the fishing was not good at all, I went out on the river with a guide. In any

THIS BILL OF SALE made at St. John's, in the Province of Newfoundland, dated this 16th day of July, 1993.

BETWEEN: **CRAIG L. DOBBIN**

                (hereinafter referred to as "Dobbin")

                OF THE ONE PART

AND: **HARRY R. STEELE**

                (hereinafter referred to as "Steele")

                OF THE OTHER PART

WHEREAS Dobbin has caused to be constructed a lodge at Adlatok River, Labrador (the "Lodge");

AND WHEREAS Dobbin wishes to transfer the Lodge to Steele to be his absolutely;

WITNESSETH that in consideration of mutual friendship and the sum of One Dollar ($1.00) now paid by Steele to Dobbin, Dobbin hereby assigns, transfers and conveys the Lodge to Steele absolutely and forever.

IN WITNESS WHEREOF Dobbin has hereunto his hand and seal subscribed and set the day and year first before written.

SIGNED, SEALED AND DELIVERED
by Craig L. Dobbin in the presence of:

                           CRAIG L. DOBBIN

The agreement by Craig Dobbin to sell Adlatok to Harry Steele, witnessed by President George H.W. Bush.

event, we got to this one place, and the guide said, 'There's a really big salmon right over there.' He said that there weren't any other salmon around; there's nothing around so let's see if we can get him. I must have been there for an hour and a half.

"I would cast the line, and I couldn't see the salmon, but the guide would say 'He's just moved and he's getting interested.' So I spent about an hour and a half trying to get this bloody salmon

Harry Steele, Paul Martin, and Greg Baikie announcing the sale of Universal Helicopters to a partnership of the Nunatsiavut Group of Companies, Tasiujatsoak Trust, and CAPE Fund, a deal organized by Mr. Martin.

interested, and the guide, who I never really knew if he was leading me on or not, would lead me to three or four casts, saying, 'Okay, put it over there and he's interested in it.'

"After about an hour and a half, my arm was killing me, but I threw the line out, and I could see a distinct ripple at the fly, and we thought he was coming for it. So, I brought in my line and as I was about to throw it out, which was going to be the cast where I was going to catch it when all of a sudden above my head was this enormous noise and clatter, and my salmon took off, never to be seen again. I looked up, and there was Harry and Craig in a helicopter. They came over and were above my head, and they scared my bloody salmon off!"

Bank presidents visited the camp. Brian Porter, the CEO of Scotiabank, visited the camp often, in the company of the regional vice-president of the bank, Randall (Randy) Hartlen, who had handled all the Steele family banking business for almost forty years.

Porter's visits to the camp allowed him to meet with one of the bank's top regional customers, but it was also a time to relax, and the bank president enjoyed Harry's conversations, sitting in the wilderness away from the pressures of Bay Street.

"He would ask very thoughtful, penetrating questions, and he got a lot out of those fishing trips," says Porter. "It was business for Harry, Harry was all business but he wanted people to have a good time, and it was all about friendship and camaraderie; he was a really nice person to be around."

That proves that the Steele family fishing camps are not merely places for recreation; they are a key part of the overall business strategy. They are something unique and, of course, the fishing provides a tie to the family's roots.

Greg Baikie looks after the fishing camps, and that includes flying people in. Greg learned to fly a helicopter at a flight school in Oshawa, Ontario, more than forty years ago. He has been involved with Harry and the Steele family almost as long.

The Steele helicopter is a Bell 407. It carries six passengers and one pilot and has a range of almost five hundred kilometres. Goose Bay is the base where Greg picks up guests and supplies for the camp. Flying at 125 knots, or around 225 kilometres per hour, the 160-kilometre flight from Goose Bay to Adlatok takes forty-five minutes.

When Harry first picked up the camp, he flew there with Greg, who along with being a helicopter pilot is a licensed fishing guide. "Harry and I went up to Adlatok and looked at it and sized it up. We really didn't fish it in earnest, but once we got proper control of the camp, which was left dormant for a couple of years, we saw a bigger potential. I was still working for Churchill Falls, and they said, 'Why don't you come back, and we'll allocate this aircraft that he has in his name to the camps for the summer, and we'll make something of it.'

Harry and his grandson Eric in Labrador.

Greg Baikie, Harry Steele's helicopter pilot, in Labrador.

The chopper, Greg, and Harry in his trademark red fedora.

The fishing season runs from mid-June to the end of August including preparation and closing the place up. Guests are only there from the first of July until the twentieth of August.

"The fish don't come until that time, and they're only in the river where they're fit to catch, all fresh and silvery for those few weeks, Atlantic salmon, all Atlantic salmon, nothing else," says Greg.

"We'll work in the south before we even open up our camps. That was a tradition between Harry and Craig Dobbin and Craig's pilot, Henry Blake, who now fills that role as a guest. Harry is very loyal to Henry because they spent a lot of time together."

These days, Greg works with the Steele family camps, including Rob Steele's camp called Michael's River. He says there is a lot of work bringing in supplies, which is done with Twin Otters — a fairly large aircraft — which can land on floats at high tide or on wheels on a three-kilometre-long beach at low tide.

Ask Greg how he got along working with Harry, and he has a short, direct answer: "I've been with him for almost forty years now, so that speaks for itself, right?"

The people who come to the camps run by the Steele family are their guests. Some of them are accomplished fly fishermen, such as his longtime broker David Bruce, who learned the art in his native Scotland. He started going to camps in both Labrador and Newfoundland, usually for a week. He says even in the wilds of Labrador, Harry likes to be connected to the outside world, and he had the early technology to do the job.

"He was always on the phone. He had a satellite phone with him, and he had to keep in touch with all these brokers to see what was going on. He always wanted to know what was going on," says David. "Harry was very cordial. He always made sure everyone was catching fish, and he gave everyone a shot at the best pool, and there couldn't be a better host."

While David Bruce knows how to handle a fly rod, others have to be taught how to tie the fly on the line or helped to land a salmon. Wet fly or dry fly? The subject may bore non-fishermen, but it can stretch on into the night at fishing camps in Labrador. The dry fly can look beautiful, almost like something out of nature, as it lands softly on the water; its purpose is to irritate the salmon, who at this stage is not interested in food, into snapping the fly into its mouth.

Harry Steele is a dry fly man. Greg Baikie is of the other school.

"It's more of an art to present a wet fly than a dry fly. It takes a long time to learn it," he says. "Harry is a good fisherman, but I use his rods more than he uses them. He'll make three or four casts, and then something will click in his mind, and he'll have to go off and see someone. Or he'll go off talking to the guests."

Rex Murphy says that fishing is the ultimate luxury for Harry and the most important thing his business success bought him. "Harry likes to say that lots of the rich people have their big yachts, and some have their private planes and others have their great mansions, but he said that anybody who has a fishing camp in Labrador has something that none of these people have and it's the thing that people really want," says Rex.

"George Bush senior wanted to go there, the manager of the Bank of Canada wanted to go there. And he's not hobnobbing with the big powerful guys, he's observing. Speaking of his wide range of acquaintances, I ran into Mordecai Richler there. Steele is not literary, and that's not a criticism, he's just not, and I don't think Richler is a Newfoundlander, but they got on like a house on fire."

Gerry White, a longtime friend of Harry's from Gander — among other things he poured the concrete for Harry's house decades ago — made many trips to the fishing camps. He remembers an unusual incident: "We had a sheik from Saudi Arabia at the camp one time, and there was a group of us up there. The sheik had five people with him: his valet and his bodyguard and his secretary and all those people, and they were all going around saying, 'We're going to do this for the sheik and that for the

Harry in paradise, salmon fishing in Labrador.

sheik,' and Harry said, 'Listen here, I'm the sheik this weekend. We're in my place now.' And everybody had a chuckle."

It was a business trip. The Saudi was in Canada to buy helicopters and the head of Bell Textron, who knew Harry from the helicopter business, asked if he could bring his client fishing, and in this case, hunting as well.

"The sheik was an excellent marksman and a very good fellow. It was an enjoyable weekend, and Harry made it all work," says Gerry.

Eighteen

Harry, the Man

The only good thing about Friday is that
it's close to Monday.
— Harry Steele's aphorism on work

They don't call Harry Steele The Commander for nothing. It isn't just his navy background. It is hard to know what formed his character, but a poor boy from an isolated Newfoundland outport grew up to command a room like few men could. Where did that come from?

It's impossible to say, but that characteristic was one of the reasons that once he made a business success of himself in his forties he was in demand as a corporate director. That was the thing about his father that always impressed his son John, his natural charisma. When his father walked into a room, the dynamics of that room changed.

"My father was just the kind of guy who you just always knew when he entered the room. There was just kinetic energy that changed in the room, and all eyes would go to him, and he could walk into the room, and it would change. I experienced it all my life. It's not something I have, but I could see that he had it," says John.

"He never said to me that he knew he had it, ever. I don't know if that's modesty or lack of self-awareness, but there is no doubt that he had it. People wanted to meet him and wanted to talk to him; he was like a magnet."

John says there were other aspects of his father's personality that made him such a successful deal-maker. "I think that he was always upfront; there was never any hidden agenda, and he always knew that the guy on the other side of the table, it had to work for them too. He has always been accused of overpaying, but he always knew that it had to work for everybody for it to be a good deal. He was never a bottom-feeder."

Roy Rideout worked for Harry at EPA, and then at Newfoundland Capital Corporation. He can't quite put his finger on what makes Harry run. "I've known Harry now for forty years, and I've never figured him out. He's a man of contradictions. Catherine has said that to me, and I nodded my head but didn't share my thoughts with her, but she said he'd do things that were totally contradictory to other things he'd do. He is very generous, but he didn't delegate generosity at all. As an employee running one of his companies, you had to spend your money like it was coming out of your own shallow pocket. He runs a tight ship, cost-wise, but he paid his key people generously, probably more than he needed to.

"He's an in-charge guy, and you could see the military in Harry, even in the way he dressed and so on. He was a great listener; he was always attentive and watchful. He controlled all the shares of the company so he could appoint anyone he wanted to the board of directors, but he never picked any yes men. He always had great boards: CEOs of big companies, like Rowland Frazee of the Royal Bank, and Bob Bandeen of Canadian National. He hired strong guys, and he listened to them even though he was an in-charge guy.

"When he made me the president of NCC, he had a committee of the board that talked to three internal candidates. I wasn't expecting to be the one at all; in fact, I told him that. I asked him 'Harry, why are you doing this?' I said, 'You own the

Harry with his one frivolity: the red Ferrari.

company, and you're in charge, and you know us better than the board.' He said, 'Oh no, I'm listening to the recommendation of the board, and that's it.' So I never quite entirely figured him out. He's a really tough, ballsy guy — I mean during that strike (at EPA) he never backed down — but he had great difficulty dealing with a loyal soldier who wasn't cutting it. I guess that was a sign that he had a big heart inside a pretty gruff [exterior], but if you got him mad, look out. He did not tolerate laziness or dishonesty at all. Mistakes were quickly forgiven if you made them honestly."

Roy Rideout says that though Harry was tough, the image belied a softer side. When it came to firing people, Roy was the hatchet man. "Human resources, hiring and firing, and motivating the presidents of these companies was the hardest part of it all. Harry was a pretty tough guy, he was a man of contradictions, but he didn't like the really tough personnel things. He had a big heart and maybe my heart wasn't as big as his," says Roy.

"These guys reported to me, so if something had to be done, I had to do it. Harry never asked me to do something I didn't want to do. I was usually the one who went to him and said, 'Harry, this is not working' and get his okay. He never said, 'Rideout, you're going to have to get rid of that guy.' He found it personally difficult to do these things, he really did, which kind of surprised me … but he's a very human guy as well."

Harry Steele was always very frugal, unlike his best friend, Craig Dobbin. In Gander, Harry and his wife live as they do in Dartmouth. In Florida, he drove an old car; in Dartmouth, a dated Subaru; and in Gander, a Range Rover that was well past its sell-by date.

He owned a modest condo in Clearwater, Florida. When his wife, Catherine, said she might like something larger, his sons had to talk him into it. His one big splurge was a red Ferrari 308, which he bought in the early 1980s, along with a red fedora to go with it that became a kind of Harry trademark.

Rob Steele says many traits made his father a success. Some of them are what you would expect: discipline, hard work, and clean living.

"He didn't have very many bad habits, not a drinker, not a party guy — very focused, an early riser, and a lot of energy. He'd get up at 5:30 or 6:00, sometimes earlier. I don't ever remember him being in bed past 7:00 in the morning.

"He is the opposite of a procrastinator; he deals with stuff immediately. And he's not a grudge holder," says Rob sitting at a table in Gander with his brother John. "If he had a problem with you, me, or Pete, or anybody, he would let you know in the moment, tear a strip off you, and that would be it. He lived in the now, and he moved right on."

Harry's training in communication and secrecy stayed with him all his life. He was a natural collector of information. He read papers, magazines, and reports, and he probed in conversations. Playing the role of the country boy from Newfoundland, he disarmed people, who would tell this jovial man things they might have kept to themselves.

One of the people who noticed this trait was Doug Rose, who wrote speeches with Harry, travelled with him, and watched The Commander at work when it seemed like play.

Harry believed information was king. He was in intelligence in the navy, so he knew the value of information and the importance of networks. He never lost track of people. He could go back and talk to pilots from EPA, when they weren't on strike, as easily as he could speak to Conrad Black, Paul Martin, or George H.W. Bush.

"He never lost track of old friends or colleagues, and he always had time to talk to them," says Doug. "He'd ask 'What's new, what's on your mind, what's going on.' He had that kind of appetite for information and was always trying to find out what was going on with the people."

When you are sitting on a frigate out in the North Atlantic, the job is to listen for Russian traffic, not have the Russians listen to you. Harry took that lesson with him as well.

"When people were talking too much, he would say, 'You know people would be well advised to go on receive sometimes rather than transmit.' He was a guy who did a lot of listening," says Doug, who listened to Harry quite a bit, absorbing ideas for speeches and the like.

"Try to ask him what was on the go on his side, and he would say, 'Well, not too much.' Next subject. He was a pretty good listener and a pretty good information gatherer.

"He had an unusually high ability to be very dynamic and action-oriented; he'd take in a lot of information from a lot of people, and he had a voracious appetite for information. He read every newspaper he could get his hands on in the morning and he'd be carrying around all the journals in his case," says Doug.

Once, on a plane trip back from a fishing camp, a banker commented that Harry had just spent time with a group of top business people, but spent forty-five minutes talking to a fishing guide. It was a snobbish observation perhaps, but Harry had a quick answer: "You'll learn as much from one as the other."

"He was perceptive; he saw things for what they were, and he was a realist. He never lost track of which shell the prize was under. He would see through the guise of a deal very quickly, and where the value of it was once you gave him the facts. He was quick.

"Harry had a consuming interest in leadership, and I don't mean that in an academic sense," says Doug. "He was a true leader of people. He knew how to pick the best people and how to rely on their best talents to get things done. He was interested in what it meant to be a leader and how it contributed to the success of the operation. He often lamented about the dearth in leadership, whether it was in politics or business or the communities. He used to often say to me, 'No wonder they can't get anything done; they don't have any leadership.' He took his experience from the navy with him and used it wherever he went.

"Along with leadership, he was interested in how to keep people motivated, which may be too formal a word. He was interested in how to build energy, how to get things done. The aura Harry always exuded was one of a ton of energy and bigger than life. People who met him said that instead of taking energy from you he always gave you energy. Everybody who worked for him was very loyal to him. Harry was the kind of a guy whose leadership was infectious and boundless.

"Harry valued loyalty above many other things. He was extremely loyal to all the people that worked for him and those people, in turn, returned that loyalty to him. He would help anybody who he thought needed it. If he thought you were in trouble, he'd find a way to help, and he didn't just do that for the people who were working for him then; he kept contact with people back through his career and reached out and helped them in every way he could. A lot of people don't know that about him, but that's what he did."

Doug Rose remembers sayings Harry sprinkled into his conversations. "I remember telling him, 'We have to be careful, Harry, that we don't spend too much money,' and he said, 'Rose, you can't save your way to prosperity.'

"That gives you a good indication of his personality. He was cautious, and he was careful, and he hired all the right help to tell him things, but he knew at the end of the day that you couldn't sit on your shekels and count them and make money, so you can't save your way to prosperity.

"Another one [of his mottos] was, 'Take cookies while they are being passed.' When you think about that, a lot of people don't take the time to remember that, but when there are things on the go that are good, take them and do what you can and enjoy them. It reflects in my mind the opportunist side of him. If things are going well, well, enjoy it and take the cookies while they're being passed."

Scott Weatherby worked with Harry Steele from the year 2000 and was always impressed with his work ethic and the need to be "on deck," leading by example. "Harry Steele was an imposing force, very decisive, in command, and in control, and always wanted to know what was going on. He took the time to stop and talk to people; he really enjoyed talking, as it was how he gathered information and [how he was able to] really understand what was going on. He liked to know what was going on in his businesses right down to all the levels," says Scott.

"As a businessman, he was very firm and wanted to get results. He always strove to hire strong people and was never intimidated by hiring smarter or stronger people than him. He often said that you had to have a smart team around you but you [should] never have people around you that outwork you, so he was always the first one here in the mornings. Even in later years, it was nothing for him to be here first in the mornings and nothing for him to take a red-eye, go home and get changed, and come in to work. It was very important to him to be in the office and working hard."

People may call Harry Steele The Commander, but once he left the navy, he put that life behind him. His son John says his father never spoke that much about the navy and John can't recall if he ever mentioned having a favourite ship. "If he had a favourite ship, he never talked to me about it over the years. He was a very singular guy. In his mind, he was starting his career late, so he had to concentrate on that. In some ways, he's a funny guy, but he's a super intense guy and a guy who didn't have any hobbies. He looked upon people who wanted to golf or sail with great disdain," says John. As to which of his sons has the father's personality: "I think different people will look at different aspects of him and apply [them] to us in different ways. I think in a business mode people will see Rob be more like him; I think in some mannerisms, and physical resemblance people will attribute some of that to me."

There were many different businesses Harry owned over the years, but he didn't run them, according to John. For him, the part of the business he liked was sizing up an opportunity and doing a deal. There were exceptions, of course. He was deeply involved in EPA, and he always had a soft spot for the hotel business and the people who work in it.

"He's not an operator, so it doesn't matter what kind of business it is. I think he and Rob are much alike; they're not operators — so as long as they are doing deals and it's making money. Whatever the opportunity was, he was going at it — selling widgets or picking blueberries. He just basically did the deals on them, and the operators reported into him. He never looked at me misty-eyed talking about Clarke or Halterm or anything like that."

When Newfoundland Capital was sold in 2018, the only business it had left was 101 radio licences. A lucrative collection and one that fetched $508 million. But Harry couldn't have cared less about radio, or at least the workings of it.

"In my mind, he didn't really like radio, but he got into it because he thought it was an easy business. Coming from the military, the creative side of the business didn't sit well with him. Radio has a lot of good people in it, but it has a good number of bullshitters and blowhards in it too, so that used to drive him nuts," says John, who does like the radio business.

Scott Weatherby agrees. "Mr. Steele was very come-in-early-and-work-late, and artistic people are very come-in-late-and-be-creative. It's just a different way of working, which just didn't compute to Mr. Steele, and to some degree to me as well. To me, the harder and longer you work, the better you are going to do at your job, and creative people just don't seem to have that same philosophy," says Scott. "So there was a disconnect there, and he didn't build strong relationships with anyone in radio because they weren't his type of people.

"Rob was the opposite. He understands all types of people. Rob would have a bigger picture of the value of different people, like there are different players on a baseball team and he would understand that everybody would have to have a different skill set in order to be successful. He understood that just having a bunch of people working hard all day long doesn't necessarily make you successful; you need all sorts of traits and attributes to make the company grow."

John Steele says his father likes and understands the people who work in the family's hotel business. "I think the hotels are probably the business that Dad is most emotionally connected to. He probably could have got out of it about twenty years ago and done okay with it, but emotionally he couldn't bring himself to do it. It's the only business that he let his emotions dictate to him. The only other one that might have but didn't even come close was when he sold Universal Helicopters. He found that hard because he used to like piddling around there and he liked the people he had in the company."

John says his father is loyal to the people who work in the hotels. You can see it over breakfast at The Albatross. The people serving him treat him with great respect and he is fond of them, in a quiet way.

"There are a lot of people there with longevity, and they are good solid character people who Dad likes. They work hard — no flash, get the job done. Those kinds of things appeal to him, and those people were very loyal and have been with him for a long time. He likes that, and he's very emotional about that, and as a result, he couldn't pull the trigger on a deal that could have happened years ago, and he would have done alright with it. Also, it was The Albatross in Gander that enabled him to lever up and get EPA. So, the start of it was The Albatross, but the game-changer was EPA.

"The reality is the hotel business was a success because of my mother, not my father. She was involved in the operation of it, and she is very much the unsung hero in all this. He always got the accolades and the public recognition, but I remember at the start, being a kid, she'd be picking out drapery and bedding, all the while carrying me around, and she was very much involved in the day-to-day of that."

Banking

> *Don't ever put me in a position of saying*
> *no to that man.*
> — Scotiabank CEO Brian Porter to the
> banker covering Harry Steele

Harry Steele banked with the Bank of Nova Scotia for almost all his long business career. The man who covers the Steele interests for Scotiabank is Randall Hartlen. Most people call him Randy, but when Harry learned his formal name was Randall, he called him Randall from then on. The two men lunched often and spoke on the phone almost every day as part of Harry's daily round of calls to keep in touch with what was going on in his world.

"I've known Harry for thirty years. I've been his banker for twenty-five," says Randall. "He had just sold EPA and had moved to Nova Scotia and, as Harry would say, he had twenty-five million dollars in his jeans and he started Newfie Cap."

Randy Hartlen oversaw every detail of Harry's banking life, and that grew to include those of his sons and their business interests. "We bank all aspects of the Steele family and have for a long time. Harry crossed over from being a client to being a friend fifteen years ago or so. My dad died twenty-five or thirty years ago now and Harry has been like a pseudo-dad to me. So that's why we were tight. It was not just about business," says Randy.

"Harry is an amazing man. The Bank of Nova Scotia has opened its safe for Harry Steele and has for a long time. Harry is a man of his word. The paperwork was nice to have but you didn't need it and we don't see many clients like that."

There were periods when things at Newfoundland Capital were a bit rocky, perhaps the worst period being in the early 1990s when the Bank of Canada jacked up interest rates in part to deal with a real estate bubble in Toronto. That hurt business across the country. It was a period where you might have to count on a banker to survive.

"Harry made mistakes but he just made more right decisions than wrong decisions," says Hartlen. "The thing is that because it was Harry Steele, people were very patient if he got in trouble. And I'm not just talking about the Bank of Nova Scotia but within the finance community, you were very patient with Harry Steele because you knew he would do everything he could to turn it around. That's what happened when he got in trouble in the early 1990s.

"I forget the exact number now but it was some tremendous amount of money that they had lost. And nobody blinked; they just said, 'Give him some time, he'll figure it out.' In the next year, he only lost half as much. I remember that and everybody said, 'See, he's in recovery.' But again, Harry Steele was going to do everything he could to right the ship, so what more could a bank or financier do? Nothing. He wasn't going to disappear on you. That was part of his longevity and his success: people had so much confidence and faith in the man. Results would come and go but Harry Steele was always going to be there."

Being in touch with the banker in Halifax was one thing, but Harry's banking connections stretched across the country, from his seats on the boards of prominent Canadian companies, to his political connections. One of the people he spoke to every month was Brian Porter, the CEO of the Bank of Nova Scotia.

"I've known Harry for twenty-five years as a customer of the bank and as a high-profile business person from Atlantic Canada, and I have always held Harry in the highest regard. You can see his navy training in how he operates. He's just an absolute straight shooter and has an ability to size people up in character very quickly. He operated his business with instinct and gut; he was a very savvy businessman and a good friend of mine. We spent a lot of time salmon fishing in Labrador over the past twenty or twenty-five years, which I always looked forward to and thoroughly enjoyed. Not just the fishing but the conversation and the camaraderie. Harry is a unique guy," says Porter.

Brian came from the investment side of the bank, so he could talk about markets, one of Harry's favourite topics. He was also able to talk about another subject dear to Harry's heart: politics. Brian Porter is a Maritimer, so the two men were on the same wavelength.

He refers to Harry as the perfect customer. "He just wanted to know that we were there and we'd be supportive. Harry's view was, 'I'll never embarrass you, and in return, I never want to be embarrassed.'"

There was an understanding and a mutual respect between the two. Harry, of course, recognized the importance and power of Porter, but the banker also knew the force of Harry's will. Porter once quipped of his business relationship with Harry: "Don't ever put me in a position of saying no to that man."

Fortunately, that situation never arose. Harry made sure that his dealings with the bank, as with others, were mutually beneficial. "He was very fair and wasn't the type to take the last nickel off the table in terms of a negotiation over a loan or something like that. He was just very fair and he always took a long-term approach. Harry, like a lot of successful people, was always thinking about his business three, five, or seven years down the road, not just the next quarter," says Porter.

"Harry was a confidante of a lot of people and not just business people, politicians. Prime ministers, premiers' and finance ministers would phone Harry and ask for his advice. They did that because they valued it and they knew they'd get the straight goods," says Porter.

Randall, the banker on the ground in Halifax, agrees. "Harry Steele has a Rolodex that anybody in Canada would kill for, and Harry Steele, to this day, I'd bet you, he could pick up the phone and call anyone, including the prime minister — he has with past prime ministers, [he'd] leave a message and they [would] call him back. And do you know why? Because he's never looking for anything. I mentioned that to him and he laughed and said to me, "Randall, when I go to see someone like that, it's to say, 'Remember me, I'm Harry Steele.' When I want something, I send someone else."

How did a poor boy from Musgrave Harbour acquire those skills and that incredible charisma and the smarts?

"The answer to that is very simple," says Peter Steele. "My father had a deep hunger and thirst that manifested itself in an insatiable curiosity and inquisitiveness about everything and that was the fuel in the tank that brought him to a lot of things. That, combined with his physical stature, a man about six foot — not to put too fine a point on it but he was an intimidating man.

"When he was younger, he was one of those guys who ... would [make people do] a double take. Not because he had Cary Grant type of looks, but because he was one of those people who, when you looked at him — his eyes and his face — you could feel the energy, and the energy came from this great unsatisfied thirst and curiosity and inquisitiveness."

"Harry is a true Newfoundlander," says Rex Murphy. "You have a great big house, and the only room you use is the basement where the fireplace is, and that's the gathering room. It's as cozy as hell. Likewise, I know his apartments in Florida, and I'll tell you that for a man of his means you'd expect more. There are people that I worked with at the CBC who had better condos in Florida.

"I know where it comes from: he's one of the old Newfoundland stock who came up the hard way and hasn't forgotten it. What we call middle-class comfort for him is more than enough. He has the feeling that even though he has more money than other people, it doesn't have to be thrown away. On his own, spending on himself, it's hard to think of any indulgences. He does occasionally travel in high circles; he knows Seymour Schulich, for example. But apart from that — in later years, [he had] the helicopter but I think that had to do with having that camp in Labrador."

Rex related a story about Harry's secret philanthropy. "Ed Smith was a Newfoundlander who died recently, but he got in an accident about twenty years ago in which he crashed his van and ended up paralyzed. Harry didn't know Ed from a hole in the ground, but for the last twenty years, he got him wheelchairs and a van. You'll never see this in newspapers, but he does a lot of outstanding work one to one for the people he encounters. He's always giving money out that you'll never hear about, and I expect that I'm one of only three or four people who know this. He did that for Ed Smith, who was a paraplegic for his whole life. For Christmas, he'd fly down in the helicopter to see him, and he took care of the funeral and his wife. So, there's a lot of that; so, anyone who says he's a capitalist, it's bullshit. I know if I were ever in real trouble, even if I didn't know him, he might bark at you, but if I said I need a hundred thousand dollars, if it was true, he'd give it to you."

Harry was also loyal to people who stuck with him during the EPA strike. One of them is John French. He says there may have been two sides to Harry, but he only saw one. "I have no doubt that if he had to be ruthless he would be ruthless and do whatever he had to. You don't reach the kind of success he had by being Mother Teresa, so I'm sure people knew that and I'm sure some people found him to be quite gruff and a bit of a bulldog, but that's what you had to do to be as successful as he was in business. But I saw a very different side of him in terms of his personal generosity to me," says John.

"My wife and I were sports fans, and when Michael Jordan was at the top of his game, he came here a couple of times to Toronto to play the Raptors and I asked Harry if he could get some tickets and he got me and my wife some prime tickets to see Jordan play when he was at his best. It's a lovely memory that my wife, Estelle, took to her grave, and one that I will have as long as I have memory. We are also tennis players and love tennis, and a couple of times when I retired I asked him if there was any chance of getting some tickets for Wimbledon, and [he] got tickets for us to go there and see some of the best players of the day playing, and that was just something that I would not be able to do on my own. He was unbelievably generous to me and that's how I'll always think of him."

Barry Clouter managed airport operations for Eastern Provincial Airways years before Harry bought it. The first time he met Harry was under tragic circumstances: at the untimely death of his brother Howard in 1973. At the time, Harry was commander of the base at Gander and Barry's mother, Mary, worked in the kitchen at the base. Harry admired Mary; she was a hard worker, something he valued in others and demanded of himself.

"My mother worked in the restaurant side of the business. When I was living in Goose Bay, unfortunately my brother passed away at a very young age in Gander. It is still a very tragic event in our family. Harry wasn't involved in the airline business, but she worked for him at the base. I got a call from him, I had never met him, but I certainly knew about him through my mother, and my mother had a high opinion of him.

"When the word was out that he was going to buy EPA and she knew I would be working for him, she said, 'All I can tell you, my son, is that if you do your work, you'll have no trouble with Harry Steele.' And she was right. So, he called me in Goose Bay, and I had never met him, and he said, 'I'm sorry to hear about your brother and, as you know, I have The Albatross Hotel in Gander.' He knew that my three other siblings were all coming in for the funeral and he said, 'The hotel is there. You come here, and you'll have all you want, including vehicles for you.' I was taken aback because I had no involvement other than my mother worked for him as a waitress in the mess. He was just that kind of guy. He was so kind in all aspects of giving to people. That was my first meeting, so obviously it sticks in my mind. 'Whatever is needed, don't even bother to ask, go check in and you've got enough to worry about. Just get your mother straightened away and don't even worry about it.'"

Many years later, Barry worked for Harry Steele and came to know him as a businessman. "In my mind, Harry Steele was very tough in business, [but] very fair, and if he made a decision himself, he delivered the decision whether it was right or wrong. He wouldn't try to pawn it off on someone else; he'd say, 'It was my decision, and I'll live with the results.' He looked for people who wanted to work and a lot of people back when I joined the airline didn't have university degrees; he looked for people who were dedicated to the business and the customer, and there was no doubt about it, he could pick good people."

Barry was a person Harry admired and perhaps he trusted him because he knew Mary Clouter. "I think he knew the pedigree I got from my mother," says Barry. "She was a tremendous worker, and he says that to this day she was the best worker he ever had in the base, so he knew I had some pedigree, I guess."

Barry worked in commercial sales for EPA out of St. John's, so he would see Harry on a regular basis as he passed through the airport on his way to Ottawa, Toronto, or Halifax. He worked in Gander, then moved to Halifax when the head office moved. It was an employer-employee relationship, but Barry says he got to know him and the kind of man he was. He says Harry Steele is a Newfoundlander down to his boots. "No question about it, he's a Newf," says Barry, who was also born in Newfoundland. Commenting on another trait of Harry's, he notes his addiction to news and current events. "When I went in to see him in his office, you'd trip over newspapers and magazines. He was up on everything."

Barry was working at EPA during the strike, a period he describes as "terrible." He was in charge of airport operations, everything from ticket counters to work on the ramps. He says it was the force of Harry's personality that kept the airline alive during that period.

"Harry had that leadership quality that kept all the troops upbeat, and [he] never showed any weakness that I could see," says Barry. "People had a lot of respect for him. Some would call him Commander; I always called him HR, but most people would just call him Mr. Steele."

Harry Steele faced down a lot of people in his business career, but there was one incident in Gander when he came up against a man with a gun who was intent on shooting him dead, to exact revenge for some imagined slight. His son John witnessed the start of it. "Back in the early 1970s in Gander, there was a young guy who came into The Albatross, and he was white as a ghost, saying, 'So and so was over next door and he has a gun, and he said he says he's going to shoot you.'

"Dad asked where he was and I said over next door. So Dad marched right over and went right up to the guy and said, 'Hey, so and so, what's all this about you're going to shoot me?' The guy had the handgun there, and he backed right down. Later, I asked Dad if was scared, and he said, 'No, I wasn't scared because if you know anything about handguns [you know that] you have to be trained in handguns to have any type of accuracy and I knew for sure that this guy had no training.'"

Military training comes in handy.

Corporate Directorships

Harry Steele caught the eye of corporate Canada. As soon as he sold Eastern Provincial Airlines and joined the CP Air board, the top ranks of corporate directors spotted new talent. Harry went on to become a director of more than a dozen Canadian companies. A partial list, which does not include things such as CHC and Newfoundland Capital Corporation, appears at the end of this section.

Seymour Schulich learned about Harry's keen eye for markets and business opportunities and recommended him for more than one board, including Dundee Bancorp Corporation. Dundee was a holding company that had a wide range of investments, from wealth management to mines.

Its CEO was the legendary investment entrepreneur Ned Goodman, who, among other things, founded Beutel Goodman, which managed money for institutions such as pension funds and insurance companies.

The chairman of the board during Harry's period at Dundee was Harold Gordon, also known as Sonny Gordon, a Montreal lawyer with Stikeman Elliot. "Harry is a terrific human being. I honour and respect him. He's decent, thoughtful, considerate, and smart. I knew him over the years because he was from Newfoundland and I had some dealings with Newfoundland but he was appointed a board member of Dundee Corporation, and I was the chairman of that board."

Sonny Gordon says Harry Steele was an active director, not someone who flew in for meetings, collected his director's fee, and went home. "Harry was a guy who I liked and trusted; Ned liked him and trusted him. He had very good judgment, and he wasn't a showoff or anything like that. He had good, sound, practical, pragmatic advice, and we looked up to him. He was one of our strong directors.

"Harry's background, and down to earth common sense — as well as his feel for markets and opportunities — was why Dundee had him on its board.

"Harry knew everyone in Newfoundland and the Maritimes, and you could reach out to him, and he would be helpful in that regard. He is also a businessman who liked business deals, and he was smart. He was also a big friend of Seymour Schulich's, by the way, and Seymour and Ned used to be partners."

What made him attractive to these big Canadian companies that put him on their boards?

"He was not a showboat; he was a good, reliable, and pragmatic director. He was smart, he was sensitive, and he added a lot of good value to the board. I used to love going fishing with him at Adlatok in Labrador," says Gordon. "Harry is a good guy. He's valuable, he's important, and I miss my talks with him. He was a real Newfoundlander."

Tom Kierans and Harry Steele sat on the board of Fishery Products International. Tom's father, Eric, was a businessman and politician, in the cabinet of both the provincial and federal governments. Tom was head of the C.D. Howe Institute and moved effortlessly between the worlds of business, volunteer boards, and academia. He was a prominent corporate director and a serious player in the world of Canadian business.

He and Harry quickly formed a bond not on the business side, but because they shared what Kierans describes as "a perverse sense of humour." "When we sat on the board of Fishery Products together, Vic Young, who was then the CEO, had to separate us from being beside each other at the table as we were always joking around at the table, but the relationship was always a one-on-one relationship. We enjoyed each other's sense of humour.

"Fishery Products International had a licence for offshore fishing for cod. When the cod disappeared, management sent all these young men out all over the world to fishing ventures to buy fish and ship it to Newfoundland so a fish supplier could sell it to its customers," says Kierans. It was Newfoundland's largest seafood company.

Eventually, the firm was taken over by High Liner in 2007, with the fishing licences sold in a separate deal. Tom Kierans stayed in touch with Harry.

"Harry was very shrewd. He bought Eastern Provincial Airways and did very well with that, and he started up a whole series of radio stations, which his son took over. He did very well at that," says Kierans. He added that Harry was an active board member, not a rubber stamp type. "He would be involved. What made him a success? He was scrupulously honest, and he was a brick; I mean he was a very strong man, and by that I mean character."

At Canadian Airlines, it was a case of the minnow eating the whale. When Canadian Airlines International bought Eastern Provincial Airways in 1984, the company asked Harry to join the board. The big airline had lost out to Harry's masterful lobbying on behalf of EPA, so they thought it was better to have him inside the corporate tent.

When Newfoundland Capital Corporation sold its newspaper in Halifax to Hollinger, Harry was asked to go on the board of Southam, the newspaper company Conrad Black ran. Black is a big fan of Harry's, which is why he asked him to be on his board. "I had occasion to see him fairly often, and he was always extremely insightful and prescient with what he said in a business sense and an extremely convivial person. He is one of those unusual people who was very intelligent and very nice," says Black. "He was always a very reliable source of advice, just a very fine man.

"I had a very nice reunion with him a couple of years ago. We had been in touch from time to time by email. I went to a big party down in Halifax with a few friends, and he was there, and I sat with him, and we had a great reunion. We've spoken a few times since then."

Corporate Boards

1990s	Fishery Products International
1984–2000	Canadian Airlines International; appointed chairman in 1990; resigned in 2000
1990–2003	CHC Helicopter Corporation
1991–2012	Dundee Bancorp Corporation
1991–2012	Halterm Income Fund
1997–2004	Hollinger Canadian Newspapers GP
1997–2000	Dalhousie Medical Research Foundation
1997–2006	Major Drilling
1999–2003	Canada 3000
2000–2001	Inmet Mining Corporation

Order of Canada and Other Awards

Harry Steele received the Order of Canada on April 29, 1992, from the late governor general Ray Hnatyshyn. Along with the lapel pin and medal comes a short citation:

> Although he remains modest about his career achievements, this Newfoundlander had a distinguished naval career before becoming one of the leading entrepreneurs in the Maritimes. He is a generous employer and community-minded citizen whose support of various local causes in the areas of education, health care and the arts is well-known.

Harry receiving the Order of Canada from Governor General Ray Hnatyshyn.

As well as the Order of Canada, Harry received other honours and awards:

1983	Honorary Doctorate from Saint Mary's University, Halifax, NS
1998	Inducted into Nova Scotia Business Hall of Fame
2000	Inducted into Newfoundland & Labrador Business Hall of Fame
2003	Received Ernst & Young Atlantic Lifetime Achievement Award
2014	Dalhousie Ocean Sciences building named the Steele Ocean Sciences Building on behalf of the Steele family
2016	Gander Community Centre renamed the Steele Community Centre recognizing Mr. Steele, in particular, and the Steele family contributions to the community

Work Habits and (Semi) Retirement

Accolades and honours were not what motivated Harry. Neither was money, really. Harry loved work. To him, the weekends were a waste of time. He had few hobbies, apart from fishing, and though he spent more than two decades in the navy, he thought messing around in boats was a waste of productive time. He was wary of hiring anyone who liked to golf or owned a boat.

Harry Steele was always at the office on Windmill Road in Dartmouth by 7:00 in the morning. He was proud to be the first to arrive and the last to leave. The official office hours were 8:30 a.m. to 5:00 p.m. Veronica Brown, Harry's long-time assistant, usually got there a little before 8:00 so she could get his full attention if there were documents to sign or things to plan. Once the business day was underway, he was busy on the phone and speaking to others in the office.

One way he was different from many top business executives was that he did not build a moat around himself, having his assistant block calls. Quite the opposite. He asked Veronica to put all calls through.

"Dad didn't care if it was someone even just trying to sell him insurance; he would never refuse to take calls," says Peter Steele. "He had this call one time from this guy who said, 'Mr. Steele, I have a business, and I'm having some issues with people, and I'd like to get your advice on what I can do to get better people and be successful.' So Dad, as was his way, told him to come down to the office and have a coffee, and the guy came down and Dad told him, 'There are two questions that I ask people when I'm hiring and if the answer is yes, don't hire them.' The guy asked, 'What are the two questions?' and Dad said, 'Do you golf and do you own a boat?'"

At the office, he would go on walkabouts to see what everyone was up to. "He loved to circulate throughout the office and talk to the employees. Everyone knew where they stood with him but he liked to keep in touch with everyone to see what was going on and he had no problem asking questions," says Veronica. "You could never fool him; you had to give him the truth because he could read right through you with no problem at all. He was very astute, but he had a great admiration for the employees. They worked hard for him, and he appreciated that. At our annual meeting, he always gave credit for the fact that the company was where it was because of the employees."

Harry paid people well and was particularly generous at Christmas. He commanded loyalty, and it wasn't just the pay cheques. He set the pace and led by example by working hard himself. The first in and the last to leave.

He got up around 4:30 a.m. and went to bed around 10:00, though no one would call Harry after 9:00 unless it was urgent. When he was at home, he was listening to the news, talking to friends on the phone, or looking at the stock markets on his computer. He was computer literate early on. He still dictated letters and memos to Veronica, a graduate of the highly regarded St. Peter's high-school secretarial program. He answered emails on his BlackBerry. The computer, whether at home, the office, or in Florida, was his lifeline to the stock market; one might say his only addiction.

Harry Steele had none of the usual run of bad habits, and he was a light drinker, even at his beloved fishing camps in Newfoundland and Labrador, where a lot of people let their guard down and overdid it. He was in Labrador from June until the middle of August, but a lot of that was business too. He did love the place though.

"Labrador was his favourite place on the planet. Labrador is the last true frontier in North America, and it's where he felt most at peace. He had a connection to it that was very deep, almost mystical," says his son Peter. "Every year, June, July, and August, he'd be in and out, but the bulk of that time he'd be up there in Labrador."

When Rob Steele took over as chairman of Newfoundland Capital Corporation in 2000, Harry Steele still came to the office and was involved in day-to-day decisions, though he stepped back and let Rob make the strategic moves, which was into radio, not an area where Harry was naturally at home.

"He put a lot of time into his first love, the stock market. I remember him saying to me, 'Pete, look at all these symbols. Each one of these symbols represents a story about a business, people, strategy, and an entity with its own thing.' He was fascinated by the symbols and what they represented in the market.

"Business for him wasn't even about the money; for him it was about [how to] *make stuff successful* and the money was just a by-product. The reason he was involved in so many unrelated and unconnected businesses was because he loved the DNA of them. He looked at businesses as living, breathing entities that were to be understood and loved and nurtured."

As he grew older, he spent more time at his modest condo in Clearwater, Florida. Even there he was on his computer and the telephone. Veronica Brown could expect seven or eight calls a day. Relaxation was going for a coffee with his friends, whether it was in Gander, Dartmouth, or Clearwater.

Vacations?

"He could never understand why people looked forward to vacations. He enjoyed work so much that, to him, it wasn't work — it was his hobby," says Veronica. "But as time went on, he and Seymour Schulich were close friends, and Mr. and Mrs. Schulich began taking cruises and invited Mr. and Mrs. Steele to join them, which they did. The only reason Mr. Steele agreed to this, I felt, was so that he and Mr. Schulich could discuss business the whole time. So they did do numerous cruises all over the world."

Information was everything to Harry Steele. *The Economist*, the *New Yorker*, the *Globe and Mail*, the *Wall Street Journal*, and more. He would be up at 4:00 a.m. and have read all the newspapers before he got to his desk in the morning. He talked to people across the country and met the top business minds in the country at board meetings, his own and the boards he sat on. His interests were eclectic. He was pals with Mordecai Richler. Talk about an odd couple. He was a political junkie, Ottawa, Washington, St. John's, Halifax, and the world. Who was doing what? How were they messing up his country?

Those were the people he liked to speak to. When you think about it, Mordecai Richler was more than a novelist, and his political writing was what fascinated Harry. Sitting on the board of Southam gave him a chance to soak in the ideas of Conrad Black. Harry may have been an outgoing man, but he was at heart a listener. Remember his naval aphorism he often quoted to his speechwriter and friend, Doug Rose: "People would be well advised to go on receive sometimes rather than transmit."

Whether Harry was on receive or transmit, he was definitely on from the time he got up before dawn in the morning until he went to bed at 10:00.

"He was at it 24/7 except for sleep. He was consumed with business, stock markets and politics and that was pretty well it," says John Steele. "He didn't have many outside interests, so he was very focused on that type of stuff. So if you couldn't converse with him on business, stock markets or politics then he wasn't very interested in talking to you."

Luckily those three subjects interest a wide range of people, especially in Newfoundland where politics is almost a way of life. Harry's natural curiosity, which he exhibited as a boy, continued through his whole life. When he met someone, he wanted to know what was happening, what they thought; that curiosity and a love of people made his life full.

Home

Ask Harry Steele where he lives, and he will answer: "Gander. That's where I live, and that's where I vote."

Gander is a small town, population 11,688. There are people who come and go at the base, but Harry knows everyone who has been there for any length of time. One of them is Gerry White, a local contractor, who first met Harry when he poured the basement of the house that Harry owns to this day. "Harry was smart, he was honest, and he was just 'full steam ahead' all the time. There was no saying no, you were going to do it, and that was it. He was a very astute businessman, very aggressive, and a very good fellow," says Gerry.

"Harry was a great contributor to the community. There is a seniors' home in Gander, and, really wherever you look around, Harry was involved with those things; with the town, with the people, and he was just a major figure in the town."

Harry liked to keep a low profile in Gander. There were a lot of things he did and people he helped that no one knows

Harry and Catherine outside the Steele family home in Musgrave Harbour.

about. One of the only things that bears his name is the community centre that Harry helped expand. Among other things, it is home to the Gander Flyers of the Central West Senior Hockey League.

Harry was born one hundred kilometres away from Gander. Now a drive of a little more than an hour, when he was growing up, you couldn't get there from here, as people used to say. Harry Steele made his own luck in life. He left the life of a roadside labourer to go to university. He joined the naval reserve and loved the life of the navy. He married a beautiful, clever woman who was his anchor in life.

The people who worked for him later, and many of the people with whom he served on corporate boards, may have had degrees in business, but Harry was self-taught; he used off-duty hours on ships to study the stock market. He was good at it and it formed the basis of his nest egg, along with Catherine Steele's real estate deals and hard work.

All of the parts of Harry's background, the frugal ways of Musgrave Harbour, the discipline and organization of the navy, all came together when he went into business. His first venture. But EPA was a big gamble. It took a tough man to make it a success.

Harry Steele never looked back from there.

An amazing life, really, for a kid who started from nothing on the edge of the cold North Atlantic in tiny Musgrave Harbour.

Acknowledgements

Many people helped me write this book. Harry and Catherine Steele were open and generous with their time on my trips to Gander. The staff at The Albatross made my stay there enjoyable. Rob Steele first approached me to write a book about his father and the introduction was made by Conrad Black, and I owe thanks to both of them. Peter Steele and his brother John helped with the history of the Steele and Thornhill families. Roland Thornhill, Catherine's brother, provided details of Harry's early investment career.

Toronto stockbroker David Bruce also shared his knowledge of that area, and Seymour Schulich was generous with his time, providing details of Harry's business life. Bill Shead, his fellow naval officer from HMCS *Fort Erie*, had some insights on the start of Harry's business career and he also pointed me in the right direction for his years in the military as did Reid Nicholson and Captain Ted Kelly.

Rex Murphy provided me with the views of a fellow Newfoundlander over lunch in a Chinese restaurant. In Gander, I was helped by Greg Baikie, Rex Avery, and Rex Primmer, who took me to see Harry's childhood friend, Beaton Mouland. Gerry White helped on life in Gander. Raoul Andersen provided stories of Captain Arch Thornhill's life at sea. An extensive article by David Napier from *Atlantic Business Magazine* was invaluable, as was an excerpt from an earlier work by Halifax writer Stephen Kimber. Kevin Griffin provided a preview of his history of Clarke Steamships.

Details of his life at Eastern Provincial Airways came from Harry, as well as his family and two pilots, Keith Lacey and John French. Further information came from extensive interviews with Doug Rose, Roy Rideout, Barry Clouter, and Tom Kierans. Kay Williams was eloquent in her description of life with Harry at Universal Helicopters as was Norm Noseworthy. David Bentley and Merv Russell provided insights into Harry's ventures in publishing and early forays in radio. Paul Martin, the former prime minister, had salmon fishing stories as well as specifics on the sale of Universal to an Indigenous group.

Scott Weatherby, the finance man at Newfoundland Capital, told of working with Harry. Randall Hartlen was Harry's banker for many years, and the CEO of Scotiabank, Brian Porter, was a staunch admirer of Harry and a companion on the river in Labrador.

Elaine Dobbin provided me with details of her late husband Craig's close friendship with Harry Steele.

Heidi Muise, Rob Steele's executive assistant, was a great help.

Veronica Brown provided invaluable assistance on an almost daily basis. She answered the phone when it rang, a rarity in this connected age, helped with meetings and introductions, suggested ideas for interviews, and spent hours poring over hundreds of photographs with me. This book could not have been done without her.

Finally, thanks to Dominic Farrell, my friend and editor at Dundurn, who made this book what it is. He is a very patient man.

Image Credits

Courtesy of Bill Shead: 24
Courtesy of Elaine Dobbin: 142, 172 (top)
Library and Archives Canada: 22, 23, 30

All other photos courtesy of the Steele family.

Index

Book Credits

Editor: Dominic Farrell
Managing Editor: Elena Radic
Editorial Assistant: Melissa Kawaguchi
Proofreader: Caley Clements
Indexer: Anna Sottile

Cover Designer: Laura Boyle
Interior Designer: Sophie Paas-Lang

Publicist: Elham Ali

dundurn.com
@dundurnpress
dundurnpress
dundurnpress
dundurnpress
info@dundurn.com

FIND US ON NETGALLEY & GOODREADS TOO!

DUNDURN